Stoic Calm

Stoic Calm

A clear guide to ending anxiety loops and moving forward with confidence

Rowan Mercer

Mindful Pages

Published in 2025

ISBN: 9789371779593 (PB)
ISBN: 9789371779685 (eBook)

Published by

Mindful Pages
Imprint of Alpha Editions LLC
312 W. 2nd St #1834
Casper, WY 82601, USA

This book was developed using advanced writing tools to support the drafting and ideation process. All content has been thoughtfully curated, refined, and reviewed to ensure quality and relevance.

Content

Introduction
The Calm in the Storm

Anxiety is a cunning intruder. Rarely does it announce itself with fanfare; it slips in quietly, cloaked in responsibility, foresight, or prudence. It tells you that replaying a conversation for the fifth time is simply being "prepared." It assures you that imagining every potential disaster before leaving the house is merely "realistic thinking." Every flutter in the chest, every shallow breath, every spike of adrenaline is interpreted as the first tremor of calamity.

Over time, this pattern ceases to be a guest and becomes the soundtrack of daily life: constant, repetitive, exhausting. Every uncertainty feels like a threat; every bodily sensation, a warning. The ordinary becomes unbearable—not because it is inherently dangerous, but because anxiety convinces us that anything could be. Trapped in a loop of hypervigilance, avoidance, and reassurance-seeking, we find escape almost impossible.

This book is a deliberate challenge to that cycle.

It does not offer another catalogue of distractions, breathing apps, or self-soothing rituals designed to "escape" fear. Nor does it promise a life devoid of worry; such a promise would be neither realistic nor desirable. Fear, properly understood, is not an enemy—it is a signal. What matters is how we interpret it, and how we choose to act in its presence.

Stoicism here is not treated as a dusty museum piece to admire from a safe distance. It is recast as a living framework for contemporary life: a philosophy forged in hardship, engineered to navigate uncertainty, and in remarkable alignment with the insights of modern cognitive science. The Stoics were not armchair philosophers insulated from the world; they were soldiers, exiles, statesmen, and teachers who trained themselves to confront chaos without losing clarity.

At its essence, Stoicism offers a deceptively simple operating system:
Control what you can. Tolerate what you cannot. Act with purpose amid discomfort.

These three imperatives strike at the heart of the anxiety loop. They reject the illusion of total control, resist feeding the machinery of avoidance, and insist on agency even amid physiological and emotional turbulence. Unlike modern anxiety frameworks that focus on symptom reduction, the Stoic approach emphasises skill acquisition. The goal is not to eliminate the waves but to become a more capable sailor.

The urgency of this approach is undeniable. In an era of ceaseless information, uncertainty is amplified rather than diminished. A constant stream of headlines, notifications, and social comparisons keeps the mind perpetually alert. Our culture rewards overthinking as diligence and treats burnout as the price of ambition. Anxiety is not merely personal—it is embedded in the architecture of contemporary life. The more connected we are, the more opportunities anxiety has to reinforce the story that danger lurks everywhere.

Yet the human nervous system is ill-equipped to manage this constant stream of perceived threats. When every unanswered message, minor bodily twinge, or ambiguous headline is treated as urgent, the brain's alarm system misfires. Here, modern science converges with Stoic insight: stress and unpredictability cannot be eradicated, but our response to them can be radically transformed.

Stoic Calm shows how. Across these chapters, you will identify the "hidden engine" of anxiety—the self-perpetuating loop that keeps you trapped—and dismantle it methodically. You will conduct a Controllability Audit, separating actionable concerns from irrelevant noise, clearing the mental fog that fuels worry. You will cultivate discomfort tolerance as a skill, learning to ride your body's alarm signals without reinforcing false messages of danger.

You will also clarify your Values Compass, ensuring that your actions align with what matters most, not merely with comfort. You will break the worry spiral—not by forcing positivity, but through targeted cognitive and behavioural strategies that intercept overthinking before it consumes the day. You will learn Stoic reframing techniques to turn looming threats into manageable challenges, and you will handle your body's alarm system with precision, not panic.

For those whose anxiety flourishes in social contexts, this book dismantles scripts and safety behaviours that perpetuate avoidance. You will approach social fears with courage and detachment from the tyranny of others' opinions. Ritual, habit, and routine will be employed to protect mental clarity amid unpredictability. Progress is measured not by the absence of anxiety, but by the presence of deliberate action.

In moments of acute stress, you will have a tested protocol—the Acute Calm Protocol—ready for high-stakes scenarios when panic threatens to dominate. These techniques are integrated into the Stoic Loop Breaker, a portable, adaptable method effective in any anxiety scenario.

This is not abstract theory. The practices presented here are grounded in case studies, real-world applications, and exercises refined in clinical, professional, and high-pressure environments. They are designed to work whether managing performance anxiety before a presentation, intrusive worries that disrupt sleep, or sudden panic surges in a crowded train carriage.

The central question is deceptively simple:
What could you achieve if anxiety ceased to signal retreat and instead became a cue for clear, decisive action?

To answer this, we must stop negotiating with anxiety as if it were rational. We must resist feeding it short-term comforts that strengthen it over time. And we must recognise that a life free of discomfort is not the measure of a life well-lived.

The Stoics understood this long before neuroscience could explain why. Control is finite, pain and uncertainty are intrinsic to existence, and courage is not the absence of fear but the decision to act despite it. Calm is no gift granted by fortune—it is a discipline, trained through repeated exposure to life's unpredictability without surrendering judgement or values.

This book offers a path to that calm. Not fragile or contingent on perfect conditions, but resilient—able to stand in the middle of the storm, acknowledging wind and rain without being swept away. A calm rooted in understanding where responsibility ends, where influence lies, and where acceptance is the only wise response.

This is not about escaping the storm. It is about becoming the person who can stand within it, steady, clear-eyed, and ready to move forward.

The work begins now.

Chapter 1
Anxiety's Hidden Engine

Anxiety rarely arrives as a single, recognisable emotion. More often, it operates like a revolving wheel, a loop that refuses to stop, despite reason or evidence. You remind yourself that the flutter in your chest is harmless; minutes later, the thought returns. You replay a conversation, convinced you handled it well, only to have doubt resurface. You postpone a decision because it feels overwhelming, enjoying a fleeting sense of relief—soon replaced by a larger, more tangled problem. For anyone familiar with chronic anxiety, this pattern is painfully familiar. Yet beneath the surface lies a hidden engine: a collection of behaviours and misinterpretations that keep the loop turning. These are often mistaken for coping strategies, but their short-term comfort conceals longer-term consequences.

Reassurance-seeking is one of the most insidious culprits. It promises control: if only you could double-check, consult one more expert, or Google one more symptom, perhaps the uncertainty would vanish. But reassurance is a fragile tranquilliser, easing tension only until the next spike of doubt. Each reliance teaches the mind that anxiety is intolerable unless externally managed. Avoidance functions similarly. Steering clear of perceived threats offers immediate relief, which the brain interprets as proof that the situation was indeed dangerous. Over time, this reward loop strengthens the very fears we hope to diminish. Overthinking masquerades as diligence. We call it "thoroughness" or "being careful," yet it is often little more than pacing in a confined space: constant motion, no progress.

At the centre of this loop is a subtler problem: the illusion of control. Both Stoic philosophy and contemporary psychology caution against confusing what is within our influence with what is not. The Stoics distinguished between what can be controlled—our thoughts, actions, and choices—and what cannot: external events, other people's behaviours, and life's inherent uncertainties. Anxiety clouds this distinction. We overestimate our power to prevent outcomes, expending mental energy on contingencies beyond our reach, while neglecting the small but decisive actions we could take. The more we struggle to wrestle the uncontrollable into submission, the more helpless we feel, intensifying the anxiety we hope to dispel.

Even the body, intended as an ally, can become an adversary. Interoception—the brain's perception of internal bodily states—plays a decisive role here. A rapid heartbeat, a sudden warmth in the chest, a fluttering stomach: all normal physiological responses, yet an anxious mind interprets them as harbingers of catastrophe. This misinterpretation is not imaginary; it stems from the brain's predictive systems. Primed by fear, the mind anticipates danger, labelling ambiguous sensations as threats. This, in turn, provokes further physiological arousal, creating a feedback loop: the heartbeat accelerates, we notice it, we panic, the heartbeat accelerates further. Without understanding and retraining this relationship with bodily signals, anxiety retains a potent hold.

Stoicism offers a striking response. Ancient Stoics faced different surface threats but the same fundamental unpredictability: political upheaval, sudden loss, illness, exile. They developed mental disciplines to navigate these realities without being paralysed by fear. Modern life presents its own brand of chaos: an unending stream of information, constant social comparison, the pressure to perform, and the sense that every decision must be optimised. We carry the world's turbulence in our pockets, delivered via notifications and headlines, while our nervous systems react as if every alert signals a predator at the door. The anxiety landscape today is not more physically dangerous, but relentless in its demands on attention and emotional resilience.

The link between Stoicism and our current predicament is practical, not merely theoretical. Where reassurance-seeking, avoidance, and overthinking offer temporary escape, Stoicism restructures how we interpret and respond to uncertainty. It rejects the control illusion, drawing a clear line between what is ours to influence and what is not. It teaches that bodily alarms are data, not commands to flee. Crucially, it reframes calm not as the absence of discomfort, but as the presence of disciplined agency amid it.

This chapter will guide you through the mechanics of the anxiety loop—not as abstract theory, but as the concrete behaviours and thought patterns that perpetuate it. You will explore why the mind clings to short-term fixes, why the illusion of control is so persistent, and how your relationship with bodily sensations can become either a stabilising force or a catalyst for panic. Finally, we will examine why Stoicism, far from being an archaic relic, remains uniquely suited to address the psychological and physiological realities of anxiety in our hyper-connected age. By the end, you will not only recognise the engine driving your anxiety but also understand where to begin dismantling it.

The Loop That Won't Quit

Anxiety has a peculiar way of teaching the mind lessons that make it more anxious. Every attempt to ease the discomfort—whether by seeking reassurance, steering clear of triggers, or thinking problems through "just one more time"—can strengthen the very patterns that keep fear alive. These behaviours feel rational in the moment. They promise quick relief, a return to stability, a sense of control. Yet, as soon as the next uncertainty appears, the need for another round of reassurance, avoidance, or overthinking arises. This is the loop that won't quit: a self-perpetuating system in which the solutions become part of the problem.

Reassurance-seeking is perhaps the most deceptively comforting of these habits. At its simplest, it involves turning outward for confirmation that one is safe, correct, or acceptable. This could mean asking a colleague to reread an email before sending it, checking with a friend that you didn't sound awkward in a conversation, or scouring the internet for proof that a bodily sensation is harmless. Each act brings a brief, tangible drop in anxiety. But relief through reassurance is like drinking salt water: it quenches thirst momentarily while making the underlying problem worse. Neuroscientific research suggests that each reassurance episode reinforces the brain's belief that anxiety is intolerable unless neutralised immediately. The nervous system learns that distress signals require instant intervention, rather than gradual tolerance. The result is a narrowing of emotional resilience: situations that once caused mild unease become triggers for full-scale worry simply because the brain has never been given the chance to ride them out without external rescue.

Avoidance operates on a similar reward structure, but instead of seeking confirmation, it opts for escape. We skip the presentation that makes our stomach churn, decline the social event for fear of awkward silences, or delay the medical appointment because the news might be bad. In behavioural terms, avoidance is negatively reinforcing: the removal of discomfort is itself rewarding. The brain records the sequence—trigger, avoidance, relief—and becomes quicker to suggest avoidance the next time. Over weeks, months, or years, the avoidance habit spreads, quietly annexing more and more of life's territory. It is rarely a conscious surrender; rather, it is an accumulation of small evasions that shrink the range of experiences we are willing to engage with. This is why exposure-based treatments in psychology insist on facing feared situations gradually: without breaking the link between avoidance and relief, the loop remains unbroken.

Overthinking, the third major player, feels more active than the other two. It masquerades as problem-solving, encouraging us to keep turning over scenarios in our minds in search of certainty. The trouble is that genuine problem-solving has an endpoint—an action plan, a decision, a concrete next step—whereas overthinking spirals indefinitely. Cognitive studies show that ruminative thought keeps the brain in a state of perceived threat, sustaining physiological arousal even when no action is taken. The body responds as though danger is imminent, while the mind remains trapped in the mental equivalent of a hamster wheel. Paradoxically, overthinking can make decision-making harder: by flooding working memory with possibilities and counter-possibilities, it leaves less cognitive bandwidth for weighing evidence or spotting obvious solutions.

These three behaviours share a common short-term logic: remove or neutralise the uncomfortable sensation now, and you will feel better. From a Stoic perspective, this is a misjudgement of what lies within our control. The discomfort of uncertainty, the presence of doubt, or the flutter of a racing heartbeat—these cannot be eliminated at will. What we can control is our response: whether we lean into tolerance or feed the loop by chasing immediate relief.

Ancient Stoics trained themselves to hold discomfort without flinching, recognising that the attempt to avoid every unpleasant feeling leads to a life dominated by them. In cognitive-behavioural terms, this is exposure and response prevention; in Stoic terms, it is the cultivation of *apatheia*—not the absence of feeling, but the ability to remain undisturbed by it.

Modern examples illustrate how insidiously the loop embeds itself. Consider the manager who habitually seeks reassurance from her team before presenting to senior leadership. Over time, her confidence becomes contingent on their approval. When they are unavailable or offer only lukewarm feedback, her anxiety spikes higher than before. Or the student who avoids participating in seminars out of fear of sounding uninformed; each missed opportunity to contribute becomes proof in his mind that he is unfit to speak, which makes future participation even less likely. Even in intimate relationships, the loop can distort dynamics: the partner who repeatedly asks, "Are you upset with me?" may find that the question itself starts generating the tension it was meant to prevent.

Breaking this cycle requires an understanding that short-term relief often trades against long-term resilience. The nervous system learns through experience, not through intellectual persuasion alone. If every spike of anxiety is followed by immediate relief—whether through reassurance, avoidance, or mental rehearsal—the body never receives the data that the feared outcome can be endured, or that it often does not occur at all. By contrast, allowing the anxious state to peak and subside without interference sends a different message: discomfort is survivable, and it does not require constant management. This is where the alignment between Stoic discipline and behavioural science becomes clear. Both insist that mastery over fear is achieved not by eliminating it, but by changing our relationship to it.

There is also a broader cultural context to consider. Modern life offers unprecedented tools for instant reassurance: messaging apps for quick replies, search engines for medical questions, and social media for public validation. These are not inherently harmful, but they create an environment in which the loop is constantly reinforced. The temptation to "just check" becomes habitual, and what was once a safety net becomes a dependency. In such a climate, the Stoic emphasis on self-sufficiency is not antiquated—it is radical. Choosing not to seek reassurance at the first sign of uncertainty, or resisting the urge to avoid a mildly uncomfortable situation, is a form of mental strength that stands against the grain of our convenience-driven world.

It is worth noting that reassurance, avoidance, and overthinking are not inherently irrational in every instance. Each can serve a legitimate function: reassurance can clarify genuine uncertainty, avoidance can protect from actual danger, and deliberate thinking is essential for complex problem-solving. The difficulty lies in recognising when these behaviours have shifted from strategic tools to default reactions—when they operate not in service of our goals, but in service of the loop itself. Developing this discernment is part of what will be explored through the Stoic and cognitive frameworks in this book.

Ultimately, the loop that won't quit persists because it offers an easy bargain: a small payment of immediate comfort in exchange for an invisible debt of long-term freedom. Most people accept the bargain without realising its terms. The work ahead is not about rejecting comfort for its own sake, but about refusing to let it dictate the boundaries of our lives. By seeing the loop clearly—understanding its triggers, its mechanics, and its costs—we create the first real opening through which it can be disrupted. And in that space, however small at first, anxiety begins to lose its automatic grip.

The Control Illusion

One of the most reliable ways to sustain anxiety is to confuse influence with control. The mind's urge to predict, prevent, and perfect outcomes creates an unspoken assumption: if we think hard enough, plan far enough ahead, or monitor events closely enough, we can bend reality to our will. Yet this assumption is flawed. We are not only overestimating our power over the future, we are underestimating the inevitability of the unexpected. The result is a constant state of vigilance—a readiness to pounce on problems before they exist, which exhausts the mind and convinces the body it is in perpetual danger.

The Stoics recognised this error two thousand years ago. Epictetus drew the line in the simplest possible terms: some things are up to us, others are not. What is up to us are our choices—our judgements, intentions, and actions in the present moment. What is not up to us includes the behaviour of others, the unfolding of events, and any outcome subject to forces beyond our command. This distinction is not an abstract philosophical exercise; it is a survival mechanism. When blurred, it produces the mental equivalent of tugging on a locked door for hours, exhausting ourselves while making no real progress.

From a psychological perspective, the control illusion is sustained by cognitive biases. The "illusion of control" bias, documented in behavioural research, shows that people tend to overestimate their ability to influence outcomes even in games of pure chance. In daily life, this translates into believing that if we word an email perfectly, we can control how it is received, or that if we monitor every minor symptom, we can prevent serious illness. This mindset is not simply optimistic—it is subtly tyrannical. It demands perfection from ourselves and compliance from the world, and when neither materialises, it fuels frustration, self-blame, and further anxiety.

Chronic worriers often operate from the belief that vigilance itself is a protective act. The mind reasons: if I keep thinking about it, I'll be ready for whatever happens. But readiness without boundaries morphs into hypervigilance, a state in which the nervous system is continually activated. Cortisol levels remain elevated, sleep quality declines, and even minor uncertainties are processed as potential threats. Over time, this constant scanning erodes the ability to distinguish between manageable problems and those beyond reach, collapsing them into one homogenous category of "things to worry about."

Modern life compounds the problem by providing endless opportunities to monitor and intervene. A project update arrives instantly; a friend's location can be tracked in real time; a news alert can deliver a crisis halfway across the world to your palm within seconds. On one level, these tools offer genuine utility. On another, they tempt us to believe that constant surveillance equates to control. This is a costly misconception. The more we try to track every moving part of life, the more data we generate to worry about, and the more reactive our minds become.

The Stoic countermeasure is deceptively straightforward: to engage fully with what is within our sphere of control and to release what is not. This does not mean apathy toward the uncontrollable—it means refusing to allocate emotional resources to outcomes that are inherently uncertain. For instance, a surgeon can prepare meticulously for an operation, refining skill and reviewing every step, but the body's healing process will still unfold according to biological realities beyond surgical control. Investing anxiety in that phase does not improve the outcome; it only drains the surgeon's capacity for the next case.

There is also a deeper psychological liberation in this approach. When we accept that control is limited, we can redirect our energy toward influence. Influence is softer than control: it acknowledges uncertainty while still recognising the value of action. A parent cannot control their child's eventual career choice, but they can create an environment that nurtures curiosity and resilience. A leader cannot control market fluctuations, but they can set a strategic direction and respond decisively to change. In both cases, the shift from control to influence prevents paralysis when reality resists our plans.

Paradoxically, giving up the illusion of total control often increases actual effectiveness. Under the control illusion, much of our mental bandwidth is consumed by counterfactual thinking—replaying what could have been done differently, or imagining every possible failure point in the future. This not only reduces focus on present actions but also fosters decision fatigue, where the accumulation of trivial control attempts leaves us mentally depleted for decisions that matter. When we narrow our field of attention to what can genuinely be influenced now, decisions become sharper, actions more decisive, and anxiety less intrusive.

Consider a corporate project manager overseeing a multinational rollout. Attempting to control every cultural variable, supply chain hiccup, and local regulation would be impossible; yet many managers try. Those who reframe their role in Stoic terms—preparing rigorously, responding adaptively, and accepting that some delays are inevitable—report lower stress and higher team morale. The control illusion is replaced by strategic flexibility, which not only preserves mental health but often leads to better results.

From a clinical standpoint, therapies such as Acceptance and Commitment Therapy (ACT) and aspects of Cognitive Behavioural Therapy (CBT) echo Stoic thought. Both encourage a focus on values-driven action while acknowledging uncertainty. In ACT, "creative hopelessness" refers to the moment a client realises that control strategies—avoidance, reassurance, overthinking—are not reducing distress in the long term. This moment mirrors the Stoic awakening: recognising that our suffering is often self-perpetuated by our refusal to accept limits. Once that recognition is made, new possibilities emerge for living with clarity and courage.

Of course, abandoning the control illusion is uncomfortable. It forces us to confront vulnerability without the anaesthetic of constant intervention. Yet discomfort here is not a sign of failure; it is the sensation of the mind recalibrating to reality. The first days of resisting compulsive checking, rehearsing, or micromanaging can feel intolerable precisely because they interrupt the loop of false control. Over time, however, this recalibration restores a sense of proportion: not every outcome is ours to direct, and that is not only acceptable but freeing.

In this way, the control illusion is not merely a personal trap; it is a cultural one. Entire industries profit from selling the promise of total control—over health, appearance, productivity, even happiness. The constant invitation is to believe that with enough data, tools, or effort, uncertainty can be eliminated. The Stoic and psychological reality is that uncertainty is permanent. The choice we have is whether to meet it with frantic attempts at mastery or with disciplined acceptance and skillful action. Only one of these leaves us lighter, clearer, and more capable of responding when real influence is possible.

When the Body Becomes the Enemy

Few experiences are more disorienting than feeling betrayed by your own body. A quickening heartbeat, a wave of dizziness, a sudden warmth in the chest—ordinary physiological events—are interpreted not as harmless fluctuations, but as signs of imminent catastrophe. For those prone to panic, the first thud of the heart can be enough to trigger a chain reaction: the sensation is noticed, labelled as dangerous, and amplified by the very fear it generates. Within moments, the body is no longer an ally carrying you through the day; it is perceived as a hostile and unpredictable force, one that must be monitored, controlled, or escaped.

This cycle is rooted in interoception, the brain's ability to detect and interpret internal bodily signals. Interoception is as fundamental to survival as sight or hearing, but unlike external senses, it operates largely in the background. A healthy interoceptive system alerts you to hunger, thirst, temperature changes, or the need to rest without requiring conscious effort. In anxiety disorders, however, this system can become hyper-attuned, registering ordinary shifts in physiology as urgent alarms. The misinterpretation begins here: a flutter in the stomach that might, in another person, go unnoticed becomes, for the anxious mind, a possible herald of fainting, illness, or loss of control.

Research has shown that individuals with panic disorder often score higher on measures of interoceptive sensitivity—they are more accurate in detecting subtle bodily changes, such as counting their own heartbeat without measuring devices. While this might sound advantageous, accuracy without balanced interpretation is a liability. The body is in constant flux; heart rate varies naturally with breathing, posture, and activity. Without a framework to contextualise these changes, heightened detection becomes a breeding ground for false alarms. The nervous system, already primed for danger, learns to treat benign signals as threats, perpetuating a state of chronic vigilance.

The escalation from sensation to panic follows a recognisable pattern. First comes the detection: a change in the body's rhythm or tone. Next is the interpretation, which in anxious individuals is often catastrophic: *this must be a heart attack, I'm about to faint, I won't be able to cope if this gets worse*. This interpretation triggers the fight-or-flight response, flooding the body with adrenaline, increasing heart rate and respiration—ironically producing more of the sensations that sparked the initial fear. Each cycle strengthens the association between bodily changes and danger, making it easier for future episodes to ignite the same cascade.

This is not purely a cognitive process; it is deeply embodied. Anxiety can alter the baseline state of the autonomic nervous system, shifting it toward heightened sympathetic activation. In practical terms, this means the body remains closer to its alarm threshold, so that even minor stressors—walking up a flight of stairs, drinking strong coffee, feeling warm in a crowded room—can produce sensations that tip over into perceived crisis. The body becomes a minefield, each twinge or flutter a potential explosion.

From a Stoic perspective, the misinterpretation of bodily signals reflects a fundamental confusion between impressions and judgements. The Stoics taught that impressions—our immediate perceptions—are not under our control; they arrive unbidden. What is within our control is our judgement about those impressions. A racing heart is an impression. The thought *this means I am in danger* is a judgement. By collapsing these two into one—by treating the sensation as proof of danger—we surrender agency to the raw signal, allowing it to dictate our emotional and behavioural response.

Modern therapeutic approaches echo this distinction. Interoceptive exposure, used in the treatment of panic disorder, involves deliberately inducing feared bodily sensations—spinning in a chair to provoke dizziness, running in place to increase heart rate—so that the individual can learn, through direct experience, that these sensations are not inherently dangerous. Over time, repeated exposure recalibrates the interoceptive system, breaking the reflexive link between sensation and catastrophe. It is a disciplined re-education of the body-mind connection, much like Stoic training aimed at neutralising the emotional sting of feared events through deliberate practice.

The challenge in real-world contexts is that the cues are often ambiguous. A skipped heartbeat after a stressful meeting may be harmless, but it feels indistinguishable from the early moments of genuine cardiac distress. This ambiguity fuels the tendency to err on the side of alarm, leading to repeated medical checks, avoidance of physical exertion, and hyper-monitoring of symptoms. Paradoxically, this monitoring increases perceived intensity: focusing intently on your breathing can make it feel laboured, just as scrutinising a mild itch can make it seem unbearable. The mind's lens does not passively record; it magnifies and colours what it observes.

Cultural factors amplify the problem. In health-conscious societies, bodily awareness is marketed as virtuous: track your sleep cycles, count your steps, monitor your heart rate variability. While such tools can support wellbeing, they also risk turning the body into a data stream to be managed rather than a lived experience to be trusted. For those with anxiety, wearable devices can become a source of constant vigilance, with every deviation from "ideal" metrics interpreted as evidence of decline or danger. The intended reassurance becomes another mechanism for sustaining fear.

Practical skill lies not in ignoring bodily signals but in interpreting them proportionately. Athletes, for example, learn to distinguish between the strain of exertion and the pain of injury, enabling them to push performance without courting harm. Similarly, those working to overcome panic must learn to recognise that an increased heart rate after climbing stairs is evidence of a functioning cardiovascular system, not a failing one. This reframing requires consistent practice, especially when instinct urges retreat.

There is also value in considering the body's sensations as neutral information rather than moral verdicts. The Stoic Marcus Aurelius reminded himself that pain is neither good nor bad—it is simply a bodily event. Anxiety's power lies in persuading us otherwise, imbuing sensations with urgent meaning they do not inherently possess. By practising a kind of mindful detachment—observing the sensation, naming it, and resisting the rush to interpret—it becomes possible to break the automatic escalation to panic.

When the body is no longer viewed as an unpredictable adversary, it can return to its rightful role as an ally. This is not achieved by eliminating sensations or suppressing awareness, but by developing a calibrated relationship to interoception. Sensations are acknowledged, placed in context, and responded to with proportionate action. In this way, both Stoic philosophy and modern psychology converge on the same principle: the body will always speak, but it is our interpretation that determines whether we hear a signal to live or a signal to fear.

Why Stoicism Fits Now

Modern life offers the illusion of unprecedented freedom while quietly eroding our capacity for calm. A person in the 21st century can speak instantly to someone on the other side of the world, monitor global markets in real time, and carry in their pocket more computing power than NASA used to land a man on the moon. Yet, for all this capability, rates of anxiety and burnout are not falling—they are rising. The paradox is striking: the more connected, informed, and equipped we become, the more psychologically overextended we feel. This is the exact environment in which Stoicism, a philosophy born in the turbulence of the ancient Mediterranean, finds fresh relevance. It offers not nostalgia for a simpler past, but a disciplined operating system for navigating the volatility of a hyper-connected present.

The defining features of our age—constant connectivity, information saturation, and performance culture—are precisely the conditions that inflame the mind's tendency to overestimate threats and undervalue what it can actually control. The Stoics lived in a world of sudden reversals: political purges, shifting alliances, military conflict, and disease without cure. They understood unpredictability not as an occasional disruption, but as a permanent feature of existence. What they developed, therefore, was not a method for controlling chaos, but for maintaining clarity and moral agency within it. This distinction matters now more than ever. In a culture that equates success with control—over schedules, public image, career trajectory—Stoicism counters with a radical proposition: *your power lies not in commanding outcomes, but in commanding yourself.*

Consider the first major anxiety amplifier of modern life: *constant connectivity*. Every digital alert, every flashing notification, every "urgent" message collapses the boundary between the external world and the private mind. We do not merely receive news; we receive it instantly, repeatedly, and often in emotionally charged forms designed to keep us engaged. The Stoics would recognise this as a near-perfect system for losing one's composure. Their antidote was not withdrawal from information but discipline in engagement. Epictetus advised that one should approach impressions—the raw data of experience—with caution, testing them before granting assent. In practical terms, this means refusing to react reflexively to every ping of the phone or headline scroll. It is the opposite of the compulsive checking that modern devices encourage; it is the cultivation of selective attention as a moral and psychological safeguard.

The second force—*information saturation*—is often mistaken for empowerment. We can research any topic instantly, compare every available option before making a purchase, and track global events in minute detail. Yet the abundance of information does not always lead to better decisions; it often leads to decision fatigue, analysis paralysis, and heightened anxiety over making the "wrong" choice. The Stoic framework resolves this by placing decision-making on a foundation of values rather than exhaustive prediction. Marcus Aurelius reminded himself that the measure of an action is not its outcome—since that lies partly beyond our control—but its alignment with reason and justice. In a world where every choice feels like a referendum on one's competence, this reframing restores perspective: the worth of an action lies in its integrity, not in its immunity from failure.

The third driver—*performance culture*—is perhaps the most corrosive to mental stability. From school rankings to quarterly targets, from curated social media profiles to the demand for "personal branding," the expectation is not merely to succeed, but to be seen succeeding. This fuels a subtle but chronic anxiety: if one's value is tied to external metrics, then every setback, criticism, or moment of obscurity becomes a threat to identity itself. The Stoic stance dismantles this by shifting the locus of worth from reputation to virtue. Seneca warned against living for applause, pointing out that public opinion is fickle and often guided by values unworthy of imitation. In modern terms, this translates to measuring one's career, relationships, and personal growth against internally chosen standards rather than the fluctuating approval of peers or algorithms.

It would be easy to mistake Stoicism for detachment, a retreat into apathy as protection against the overstimulation of contemporary life. This is a misreading. Stoicism is not about withdrawing from the world but engaging with it on different terms. It advocates full participation in work, relationships, and civic life, but without staking one's peace of mind on the uncontrollable variables embedded in each. The Stoic does not decline to lead a team, take a risk, or advocate for change; rather, they do so with a mindset that has already accepted the possibility of failure without being defined by it. This is particularly relevant in an age where fear of reputational damage or public failure can paralyse even capable individuals from acting on their convictions.

There is also a neuropsychological harmony between Stoic discipline and modern understandings of anxiety. Contemporary research shows that the human stress response is often less about the stressor itself and more about the perceived gap between demands and resources. When we believe we must control the uncontrollable—market volatility, others' opinions, macro-political shifts—the gap feels infinite. The Stoic practice of focusing exclusively on the controllable compresses this gap, reducing the volume of perceived threats and allowing the nervous system to downshift from chronic activation to sustainable alertness. This is not an abstract benefit; it translates into more consistent focus, better sleep, and a steadier emotional baseline.

Real-world application makes the relevance even clearer. A software engineer in a high-pressure start-up cannot prevent sudden pivots in company strategy, but can control the quality of their work and the clarity of their communication. A political journalist cannot ensure that their reporting will change public opinion, but can commit to accuracy, fairness, and resilience in the face of backlash. A parent cannot eliminate every risk their child will face, but can model composure, integrity, and problem-solving under stress. In each case, Stoic principles serve as a buffer against the psychological wear-and-tear of attempting to bear the weight of the entire outcome.

It is worth noting that Stoicism also has an answer to the subtle moral erosion caused by hyper-competition and constant comparison. Performance culture not only strains mental health; it can incentivise ethical compromises in the pursuit of recognition or advancement. By rooting self-respect in virtue rather than results, Stoicism offers a counterweight: better to lose honourably by one's own standards than to win by abandoning them. This is not only a moral safeguard but an anxiety-reducer—when your worth is not contingent on beating others, you are freed from the constant, corrosive calculation of whether you are "ahead" or "falling behind."

For all its ancient language and context, Stoicism aligns closely with modern evidence-based approaches to anxiety management: exposure to feared scenarios, cognitive reframing, acceptance of uncertainty, and values-based action. What distinguishes it is the depth of its moral architecture. It does not simply aim to reduce distress; it offers a philosophy of life that makes distress less destabilising when it does occur. In this way, it meets the twin demands of the present moment: the need for immediate tools to navigate daily pressures, and the need for a coherent worldview that can hold steady in the face of the century's volatility.

That is why Stoicism fits now—not as a nostalgic retreat into ancient thought, but as a forward-facing discipline for thriving amid the speed, noise, and relentless demands of the modern world. It offers a way to remain connected without being consumed, informed without being overwhelmed, and ambitious without being enslaved to the scoreboard. In an age where anxiety often feels like the default state, this combination is not merely useful; it is indispensable.

Chapter 2
The Controllability Audit

Anxiety has a peculiar way of convincing us that every problem requires immediate attention. A conversation from last week may still linger unresolved, a looming project deadline competes with concerns about global events, and a minor bodily sensation demands focus. Without realising it, we treat all of these with the same urgency, as if each were equally within our control. The effect is not merely exhaustion; it distorts perception. Problems we could actually address become buried beneath those we cannot change, while matters we can only accept end up consuming disproportionate mental energy. The Controllability Audit is designed to correct this distortion—not through vague exhortations to "let go," but by imposing precision on how we classify concerns and determine our next steps.

At the heart of this method are the Three Circles of Agency. Picture three concentric rings. The innermost circle represents Direct Control: issues entirely dependent on your own actions and decisions in the present. These are the areas where your choices produce predictable outcomes—attending a meeting, submitting a report, taking medication, preparing for an exam. Execution is everything here. The middle circle is Influence: matters where you cannot dictate the outcome but can tilt the odds or shape the process. Convincing a client to reconsider, guiding a team toward improved performance, or encouraging a friend to seek support all fall into this category. Influence does not guarantee success but allows for strategic effort. The outermost circle is Acceptance: situations beyond your control, where your actions cannot meaningfully change the outcome—the weather during a presentation, a hiring decision post-interview, or a market downturn affecting investments.

While these distinctions may appear self-evident, in practice they are rarely applied with discipline. Hours are spent ruminating over outer-circle events, imagining "what if" scenarios, and rehearsing outcomes we cannot alter. Simultaneously, we neglect decisive action in the inner circle, where genuine impact is possible, because our attention is consumed by matters beyond our influence. This is the Blurred Zone—a fog of mental clutter that thrives on ambiguity. Anxiety flourishes here: if the mind cannot distinguish whether a concern belongs in Direct Control or Acceptance, it defaults to treating it as urgent and solvable, triggering endless cycles of checking, monitoring, and worry.

The cost of existing in the Blurred Zone is tangible. Decision fatigue mounts as issues are repeatedly reassessed without resolution. Procrastination increases, not from laziness, but because uncertainty renders engagement mentally costly. Physiologically, the body remains on high alert, ready to confront a threat that may not even be yours to manage. Over time, a subtle erosion of agency sets in: effectiveness diminishes not from lack of skill or effort, but from misallocated energy.

The Controllability Audit offers a remedy. It is not a long journalling exercise or a theoretical reflection; it is a rapid, decisive classification process. Faced with an anxiety trigger—a terse email, a concerning headline, a dip in fitness metrics—you ask: Is this under my direct control? If yes, act immediately or schedule the action. If not, can I influence it meaningfully? If yes, plan your strategy. If neither, it belongs in Acceptance, which requires no further mental processing beyond preparing to meet the outcome calmly. Its power lies in clarity: each concern is categorised, and each category carries its own default next step.

The audit draws directly from Stoic thought. Epictetus' dichotomy of control—distinguishing what is up to us from what is not—has been adapted into three tiers for modern life. Direct Control and Acceptance remain faithful to the original model, while Influence acknowledges the realities of interconnected environments, where outcomes often depend on shared responsibilities. Crucially, the audit does not promote passivity. On the contrary, it sharpens the will to act where action is possible and worthwhile, conserving energy where it is not.

In high-pressure scenarios, precision can determine whether burnout or sustained performance prevails. Consider a senior manager overseeing a product launch. Delays in regulatory approval

(Acceptance) are not to be fought; instead, she concentrates on optimising internal workflows (Direct Control) and negotiating with suppliers to improve delivery timelines (Influence). By assigning each issue to a circle, she avoids squandering hours attempting to influence factors outside her power, channeling effort where it produces real effect.

The audit also curbs overthinking. By formalising the point at which uncontrollable events are mentally released, it establishes a natural boundary for rumination. Once classified into Acceptance, further "what if" cycles are recognised as unproductive, prompting a shift in focus. Discipline emerges through repetition until classification becomes reflexive, allowing the mind to approach triggers not with alarm but with a filtering process: first sort, then act—or release.

What elevates the Controllability Audit beyond a productivity tool is its ability to restore proportion to everyday life. Modern anxiety inflates the significance of every stimulus: a minor delay feels catastrophic, a casual remark is interpreted as a warning, a fleeting bodily twinge becomes proof of illness. Pausing to ask, "Which circle does this belong to?" interrupts automatic escalation, permitting assessment on the merits of reality rather than perception.

The following chapter illustrates these circles in practice—across professional, personal, and physiological contexts—and demonstrates how even a 30-second audit can redirect a day from spiralling worry toward purposeful action. It examines the Blurred Zone in depth, identifies common signs of entanglement, and offers strategies to regain clarity. It also addresses the critical follow-up decisions: knowing a matter's category is valuable only if you understand the next move.

Ultimately, the goal is not a life devoid of anxiety—such a life is neither possible nor, in many cases, desirable. The objective is proportionate anxiety, directed where it prompts constructive action. The Controllability Audit achieves this: fast, clear, and repeatable until second nature. It replaces vague reassurance with tangible structure, scattered worry with deliberate agency, and exhaustion with purposeful focus.

Three Circles of Agency

One of the most corrosive features of anxiety is its tendency to collapse the boundaries between what we can do, what we might shape, and what we must simply endure. This collapse creates the impression that every problem demands equal attention, when in truth, the demands vary enormously depending on how much leverage we actually have. Without clear distinctions, our days are filled with reactive activity—half-steps toward unchangeable outcomes and hesitant engagement with matters entirely in our hands. The *Three Circles of Agency* provide a framework for reversing this pattern. They sharpen the mind's focus, clarify decision-making, and reduce the waste of energy on battles already lost or that were never ours to fight in the first place.

At the centre lies *Direct Control*: those situations where the outcome depends almost entirely on our own actions in the present moment. If you prepare the presentation thoroughly, it will be ready; if you take the medication as prescribed, you will have done your part for your health; if you have the difficult conversation with clarity and respect, you will have upheld your responsibility. The operative feature here is autonomy: the causal chain between your effort and the result is intact. The value of identifying this circle is that it gives anxiety a tangible outlet—when you know something is within Direct Control, the only rational next step is execution. Yet many people, paralysed by more distant concerns, fail to act even in this sphere, allowing solvable issues to fester while they worry about events far beyond their reach.

The second circle is *Influence*, and it requires a different mindset. Here, you can affect the odds, shape perceptions, or improve the conditions for a desired outcome, but you cannot guarantee it. A teacher can design an engaging curriculum to encourage student participation but cannot ensure every pupil will be motivated. A lawyer can prepare a compelling argument yet cannot dictate the judge's ruling. In these cases, the productive stance is one of strategic effort combined with flexibility: invest your resources where they are most likely to tip the balance, but accept that the final say rests elsewhere. This distinction matters because anxiety often treats influence as if it were control. We exhaust ourselves trying to "make" others decide, behave, or feel a certain way, when in reality, all we can do is create the most favourable conditions for them to choose it themselves.

The outermost circle, *Acceptance*, is the most challenging for the anxious mind to honour. It encompasses events over which we have no meaningful leverage, regardless of effort. The weather on the day of an outdoor event, the market's reaction to geopolitical shocks, or the decision of a hiring committee after the interview process—all belong here. The instinct to ruminate over such matters is powerful, because the mind is reluctant to admit defeat; it would rather run endless mental simulations in the hope of discovering a loophole. But there is no loophole in true Acceptance. The practical work is not in changing the outcome but in preparing to meet it without being unmoored. This does not mean passivity—it means readiness, which is active, deliberate, and rooted in the recognition that energy spent on the unchangeable is energy stolen from what you can move.

Understanding the distinctions between these circles is not enough; the application must be precise and rapid. In real life, anxiety does not announce itself with a pause for classification. The email from a client, the breaking news alert, the flicker of discomfort in your chest—these land unfiltered, pulling you toward reaction. The discipline is to pause and ask: Which circle does this belong to? If Direct Control, act now or schedule the exact moment to do so. If Influence, decide on the one or two interventions that will make the greatest difference and let the rest go. If Acceptance, stop allocating further mental processing beyond necessary preparation. This triage process is not about suppressing feelings—it is about assigning them to the right context before they dictate your behaviour.

Examples clarify how the framework works under pressure. Imagine an airline passenger learning their flight is delayed due to weather. Direct Control: recharging devices, notifying contacts of the new arrival time, securing an earlier seat if available. Influence: politely requesting the airline to rebook via another route. Acceptance: the storm itself and the delay length dictated by safety protocols. Without the circles, frustration over the storm might consume hours of restless pacing; with them, energy moves quickly to tasks that are actually achievable, and the rest is mentally closed off. Or take the case of a project lead whose team is missing deadlines. Direct Control: clarifying expectations, providing necessary resources. Influence: fostering accountability, motivating team members, offering solutions. Acceptance: individual team members' personal circumstances or skill limitations that cannot be changed in the short term. Here, the framework prevents the lead from spiralling into resentment over factors they cannot alter, allowing them to focus where progress is still possible.

Philosophically, the Three Circles refine the Stoic dichotomy of control. The original model drew a binary between what is up to us and what is not; in the modern context, the category of Influence acknowledges the complexity of a world in which most outcomes are partially shared. This additional layer reflects not a dilution of Stoic clarity but a tactical adaptation for interconnected systems—workplaces, relationships, economies—where influence, while not decisive, is often worth pursuing. At the same time, the core Stoic warning remains intact: to spend your life striving for omnipotence over the uncontrollable is to waste it.

The discipline of using the circles consistently has secondary benefits. It reduces the "ambient noise" of low-level worry by making decisions about where to place attention early and explicitly. It encourages decisive action in Direct Control matters, rather than letting them be drowned out by speculation about outer circles. And it builds tolerance for uncertainty in Acceptance by giving the mind a structured way to disengage, replacing the vague command to "stop worrying" with a concrete classification that justifies doing so. Over time, this classification becomes a reflex, operating as a filter through which all new challenges pass before emotional investment is made.

What makes the Three Circles of Agency more than a neat diagram is that they are meant to be lived in motion. They are a habit of mind, a continual audit of where you stand in relation to the shifting realities around you. In anxious states, this habit interrupts the reflex to treat every problem as if it were Direct Control; in calmer states, it sharpens the efficiency with which you act. The framework respects both the limits and the possibilities of human agency, which is why it stands as one of the most powerful tools for reducing unnecessary anxiety while maximising meaningful impact. When practiced deliberately, it transforms not only the way you think about challenges but the speed and precision with which you meet them.

Avoiding the 'Blurred Zone' Trap

Anxiety thrives in ambiguity. When we are uncertain whether a situation is within our control, our minds treat it as if it could be—and that "maybe" is enough to keep mental engines running at full throttle. This is the Blurred Zone: the space between certainty of control and certainty of powerlessness, where the mind oscillates between plans, doubts, and imagined scenarios without ever settling. It is in this grey territory that people burn through their cognitive and emotional reserves—not in responding to what they can change, nor in making peace with what they cannot, but in wrestling indefinitely with the uncertainty over which category a problem belongs to.

The Blurred Zone is costly because it combines the stress of a problem that feels urgent with the paralysis of one that feels unsolvable. Consider the common experience of waiting for medical test results. You cannot influence the outcome—the sample has already been taken—but you can influence how quickly you receive it by calling the clinic. Once that call has been made, however, there is no more meaningful action to take. Yet many people remain mentally tethered to the situation, revisiting it every few minutes, checking their phone compulsively, running through catastrophic interpretations of possible results. This is a textbook Blurred Zone loop: the uncertainty over whether *more* action might help keeps the mind from disengaging, even when the actionable portion is over.

In professional settings, the Blurred Zone often masquerades as diligence. A project manager receives ambiguous feedback from a client: "We'll get back to you soon." Is this an opening to follow up and clarify, or would further contact appear pushy? Instead of making a clear classification—either influence the outcome now or step back until the client responds—the manager runs mental simulations throughout the day, crafting and discarding potential messages, imagining both positive and negative replies. No actual progress occurs; the work is purely internal, but it drains energy as if hours of real labour had been done. The client remains silent, and the manager is exhausted, not from effort that mattered, but from sustaining the cognitive tension of indecision.

This is why *clarity of controllability* is as important as controllability itself. The human brain dislikes open questions. Unresolved uncertainty acts as a cognitive irritant, prompting repeated mental checking. Neurological studies of the "Zeigarnik effect" have shown that incomplete tasks occupy more mental space than completed ones, even if those tasks are trivial. In the Blurred Zone, the "task" is the classification itself—deciding whether something is worth further action—and until that decision is made, the brain continues to cycle. The consequence is that you can spend more total energy *thinking about* a situation than it would have taken to resolve it or release it.

The trap is deepened by the fear of "missing something." People hesitate to move a problem into the Acceptance category because they worry they will overlook a small but crucial action that might have made a difference. This is where the Stoic and psychological approaches converge: the only way to break the loop is to accept that acting with incomplete certainty is inevitable. The Stoic would call this trusting one's reasoned judgement in the present moment; the psychologist might call it tolerating uncertainty. Either way, the principle is the same—make the best classification you can with the information you have, act accordingly, and resist the pull to reopen the case every hour.

In practice, escaping the Blurred Zone requires two skills: decisiveness in classification and discipline in follow-through. Decisiveness is the ability to say, *This belongs in Direct Control, Influence, or Acceptance* without demanding perfect knowledge of the outcome. Discipline is the ability to stop reclassifying unless new, material information emerges. Without the second skill, the first is meaningless—you can decide a situation is outside your control in the morning and still find yourself treating it as controllable by the afternoon. The Blurred Zone feeds on this re-entry, pulling you back into the same uncertainty you thought you had escaped.

Real-world examples show the difference this makes. A team leader receives news that a budget review will be delayed until next quarter. After a moment of assessment, she decides that no action can accelerate the review (Acceptance) and shifts her focus to optimising existing resources (Direct Control). By refusing to revisit the decision each day, she avoids the mental drain of wondering whether a call to finance might change things. By contrast, a peer in another department makes the same initial classification but reopens the file mentally every time he sees the finance director, each time spending mental bandwidth rehearsing what he *might* say. The difference in cognitive load over three months is not trivial—it's the difference between mental availability for present tasks and a slow bleed of attention into the past and future.

The Blurred Zone is not always obvious because modern work and life often reward the appearance of being "on top of everything." This can lead to a performative engagement with problems that have already been dealt with. People keep checking dashboards, email threads, or shared documents not because new action is needed, but because staying visibly engaged is equated with competence. The result is a sustained background hum of low-grade anxiety—energy invested in being seen to care rather than in moving forward where movement is possible. The Stoic counterpoint is blunt: if your action cannot alter the course, it is no longer an action but a ritual of worry.

An important nuance here is that the Blurred Zone is not always a matter of failing to act; sometimes it is a matter of over-acting. Over-acting is when, uncertain of your true level of control, you attempt multiple low-impact interventions in the hope that quantity will compensate for lack of precision. This might look like sending follow-up emails to multiple stakeholders when one well-targeted message would have sufficed, or making several "just checking in" calls that do little except signal your own anxiety. Over time, this behaviour not only exhausts you but can also damage relationships, as others perceive the excess contact as intrusive or mistrustful.

Avoiding the Blurred Zone, then, is not simply a matter of thinking differently; it is a matter of instituting a habit of *single, decisive engagement*. Address what is clearly in your hands, make one strategic move in the sphere of influence, and if nothing remains, move the matter to Acceptance without looking back until real developments occur. This habit both preserves mental energy and builds trust in your own decision-making. The anxious mind often fears that without constant attention, things will deteriorate; the disciplined mind understands that constant attention to the uncontrollable deteriorates you.

By learning to spot and exit the Blurred Zone quickly, you are not just reducing wasted energy—you are reasserting control over the most important resource in anxiety management: your attention. It is attention, more than time or effort, that determines whether anxiety grows or fades. The Blurred Zone is where attention goes to die slowly; stepping out of it is how you keep that resource alive for the challenges you can actually meet.

Audit in Action

Anxiety does not arrive with a label telling you which part of it you can address. It shows up as a jolt, a knot, or a thought that feels urgent, demanding an immediate reaction. In those moments, the ability to quickly classify the trigger into one of the three circles—Direct Control, Influence, or Acceptance—is not an intellectual exercise but a practical survival skill. Without this rapid audit, your mind defaults to its least efficient mode: reacting to everything as if it were equally within your command, pouring attention into low-return areas while neglecting the actions that could actually make a difference.

The audit begins with precision. The first question is simple but decisive: *Does this outcome depend entirely on my own present actions?* If yes, you are in Direct Control. This is the smallest circle but the one that demands the swiftest response. The key here is not just identifying that you have control, but acting before anxiety has a chance to redirect you into worry instead of execution. If your stress comes from an unfinished report, the only productive next step is to sit down and work on the report—not to scroll news headlines or rehearse the consequences of missing the deadline. Every minute spent outside action in this circle is a voluntary leak of control.

When the answer is no, the second question follows: *Can I meaningfully influence the outcome?* This is not a question of mere involvement—sending a message or commenting on a thread is not influence if it has negligible effect. Influence means your input changes the probabilities, improves the process, or shapes conditions in a measurable way. Negotiating with a supplier to adjust delivery terms, coaching a team member to improve their output, or framing an argument persuasively in a decision-making meeting all qualify. Here, the audit is about identifying the single most effective move, not blanketing the problem with scattered, low-impact efforts. Over-activity is as wasteful as inaction when it comes to influence; it burns energy without moving the needle.

If the answer to both questions is no, the matter belongs in Acceptance. This is not the same as resignation; it is active recognition that no further steps on your part will alter the outcome. The mind resists this category fiercely, often because of the fear that letting go is the same as not caring. But the audit reframes Acceptance as deliberate resource allocation—you withdraw attention not because it is unimportant, but because continued investment yields no return. This is where the audit protects you from the compulsive re-entry that fuels the Blurred Zone, closing the mental file until actual change in circumstances reopens it legitimately.

The speed of this audit matters. In practice, you have seconds before anxiety starts building its own case for why the matter is urgent, personal, and solvable. Consider the example of receiving a vague email from your manager: *We need to talk tomorrow.* The immediate surge of anxiety tempts you into the Influence circle—should you send a follow-up asking for details? Should you pre-emptively justify your recent decisions? The audit interrupts this reflex. Direct Control? No—there is no task you can execute now that guarantees the conversation's content will shift. Influence? Possibly, but only if there's a legitimate reason to believe your input before the meeting would alter the discussion. If not, it falls into Acceptance, and the most effective choice is to prepare for the meeting in general terms and release the speculation. Without the audit, you might spend the next 24 hours drafting and deleting speculative responses, exhausting yourself with no benefit.

A corporate negotiation illustrates the power of the audit in more complex scenarios. Suppose you are part of a team bidding for a large contract. Certain elements—the accuracy of your proposal, the clarity of your presentation—are in Direct Control. Other elements, such as the rapport you build with the client and the trust you establish, are in Influence; they cannot guarantee the contract, but they may tip the balance. The client's budget cycle, internal politics, or pre-existing commitments are in Acceptance. The audit forces you to channel maximum energy into the controllable, strategic effort into the influenceable, and zero effort into what is fixed. Without it, you risk spending hours speculating on internal client dynamics you cannot change, while rushing last-minute corrections to the proposal that were entirely in your power to perfect.

The audit also prevents contamination between circles. Without clear boundaries, Acceptance matters bleed into Direct Control space. For example, an athlete recovering from injury might know intellectually that the rate of tissue healing is not within their control, but their anxiety leads them to over-train in an attempt to accelerate recovery—ironically increasing the risk of setback. The audit draws a sharp line: physiotherapy exercises and nutrition are Direct Control, adherence to the recovery plan is Influence (in that it creates the best conditions for healing), and the body's intrinsic healing timeline is Acceptance. Respecting those lines keeps the athlete's actions aligned with reality rather than with wishful thinking.

From a psychological standpoint, the audit works because it interrupts the default processing route of anxiety. Instead of moving from trigger to rumination, you insert an assessment that strips away the emotional colouring and focuses on mechanics: What can I do? What can I shape? What must I meet without altering? This reframing bypasses much of the catastrophising process by shifting the focus from outcome to agency. The anxious brain's bias toward "doing something" is not suppressed—it is redirected toward the highest-yield actions, which has the secondary effect of reducing overall physiological arousal.

There is a Stoic underpinning to this modern tool. Epictetus warned against investing in what is not up to us, but the audit gives that principle operational clarity. It takes the philosophical and turns it into the procedural: a 10–30 second check that categorises reality and instructs behaviour accordingly. The discipline lies not in doing the audit once in a while, but in making it reflexive—every email, every news headline, every offhand remark passes through the filter before consuming your attention.

The audit is not about being detached from outcomes; it is about being proportionate in your engagement with them. It ensures that when anxiety calls you to act, you can answer with precision rather than scattering your effort. In doing so, it transforms agency from a vague ideal into a moment-to-moment practice, one that makes anxiety a cue for clarity rather than confusion. The more consistently you apply it, the faster it becomes, until classification happens almost as quickly as the trigger arrives—and the difference between a spiralling day and a steady one becomes a matter of seconds.

Decision Points

The value of a Controllability Audit is not in the classification itself—it lies in what you do in the moments immediately after. Without decisive follow-through, even the most accurate audit becomes another form of mental rehearsal: intellectually satisfying, but practically inert. Anxiety thrives in that gap between clarity and execution, filling it with "just one more thought" or "I'll start in a minute" until the day is lost to spinning. The purpose of identifying which circle a trigger belongs to is to create a precise decision point—a moment in which you pivot from analysis to deliberate action or deliberate release.

If the audit has placed the matter in *Direct Control*, hesitation is the enemy. Delay allows the mind to turn an actionable item into an arena for rumination, where you imagine rather than act. The decisive move here is to translate recognition into immediate engagement. If the controllable task can be completed within minutes—replying to an email, correcting a document, making a phone call—it should be done now. This is not merely about productivity; it is about preventing the mind from recasting a task into a hypothetical problem. When the task is too large to complete instantly, the decision point becomes: schedule the first concrete step, with a defined start time, and clear away any competing inputs until that step is underway. Anything else is procrastination in strategic clothing.

For matters in the *Influence* circle, the decision point is about precision. Influence is a finite resource, and misdirected influence is as ineffective as none at all. The temptation is to scatter efforts—send multiple messages, drop hints to different people, or repeatedly "check in" in the hope that persistence will substitute for leverage. The disciplined choice is to identify the single highest-impact action you can take, do it, and then step back. In negotiation terms, this is making your best offer and resisting the urge to keep sweetening it unnecessarily. In interpersonal terms, it might be offering a clear recommendation, then letting the other person own the decision. Once that move is made, the audit's work is complete; lingering mentally in the Influence circle does not increase your sway, it only increases your agitation.

When the audit points to *Acceptance*, the decision point is counterintuitive: you act by not acting. This is where people often falter, because letting go feels like weakness. In reality, it is the most disciplined of the three outcomes. Acceptance is not about withdrawal from life; it is about refusing to spend attention on what cannot be altered. The decision point here is to shift attention deliberately to something within Direct Control or healthy distraction. This could mean engaging in work, physical movement, or a restorative habit that replaces unproductive mental spinning with constructive presence. Without this deliberate redirection, "acceptance" becomes a euphemism for remaining emotionally tethered to the issue, which is simply the Blurred Zone by another name.

An example from high-pressure work environments makes the principle concrete. A senior executive receives news that a major client is considering ending their contract. The audit: retention strategy meetings and revising proposals fall in Direct Control; conversations with client decision-makers are Influence; the client's ultimate strategic priorities, which may be shifting for reasons unrelated to service quality, fall in Acceptance. The decision points flow from this: work immediately on refining the proposal (Direct Control), arrange a targeted conversation with the primary contact to address concerns (Influence), and stop speculating about the client's internal board politics (Acceptance). Each point demands a different posture—execution, persuasion, and detachment—and the clarity of these distinctions prevents the executive from wasting mental resources in the wrong mode.

The transition from audit to decision point also benefits from what military strategists call "immediacy discipline"—acting while conditions are still aligned with the classification. In volatile situations, controllability can shift. A problem that is currently in Influence may slip into Acceptance if you miss the small window where your input could matter. Likewise, a controllable task may become more complex, or impossible, if left untended. The sooner you make your decision point, the less opportunity anxiety has to distort the landscape.

There is a philosophical dimension to this discipline. The Stoics spoke of *prohairesis*—the capacity for rational choice that remains ours regardless of external events. The audit is an exercise in clarifying where choice exists; the decision point is the act of exercising it. Without that act, knowledge is inert. You have drawn the map, but if you do not move, you remain lost. In this sense, the decision point is not merely a tactical tool; it is the moment where abstract agency becomes lived agency.

Psychologically, committing to a decision point also interrupts the feedback loop that sustains anxiety. Anticipatory anxiety relies on mental rehearsal without resolution—it keeps running because you have not told it, in behavioural terms, "the case is closed." When you take the step associated with your circle—execute the controllable, make the influence move, or deliberately shift attention—you provide closure. This closure is not emotional (you may still feel uneasy) but operational: you have done what can be done, and anything further would be misaligned with reality. Over time, this trains the nervous system to accept completion without total certainty, which is one of the most powerful antidotes to chronic overthinking.

In everyday life, these decision points can be surprisingly small. The parent worried about their teenager's exam performance: Direct

Control is ensuring the child has a quiet study environment; Influence is encouraging good study habits and offering help; Acceptance is the child's actual performance on the day. The decision points are equally clear: set up the environment now, offer guidance once, and then disengage from mental rehearsal of worst-case scenarios. Without the audit-to-decision process, that same parent might spend the evening asking repetitive questions, scanning the teenager's mood for signs of doom, and imagining the results weeks in advance—all of which feel active but achieve nothing.

Ultimately, the decision point is the bridge between clarity and momentum. It is the moment where you either give anxiety new material to work with or deny it that fuel entirely. The Controllability Audit sharpens perception; the decision point operationalises it. And in anxiety management, operationalising insight is everything—because thinking about control is not the same as exercising it, and knowing what you should do is worthless unless it is followed by the discipline of doing it now.

Chapter 3
Training for Discomfort Tolerance

The human mind naturally seeks the path of least resistance. When discomfort appears—whether in the form of a difficult conversation, an impending presentation, or the vague unease of social exposure—the impulse to step back, reschedule, or wait for a "better moment" feels rational. Avoidance masquerades as prudence, whispering that retreat is a calculated delay rather than a surrender. Yet repeated over time, this reflex erodes resilience. By shielding ourselves from brief spikes of anxiety, we train the nervous system to interpret discomfort as inherently threatening, reinforcing the very perception we aim to dismantle. Gradually, avoidance reshapes the terrain of our lives, narrowing social circles, curtailing professional opportunities, and quietly eroding self-trust—not through conscious choice, but through the unconscious rerouting of our steps away from anything that feels unsafe.

Discomfort tolerance, paradoxically, is not an abstract trait; it is a skill cultivated through deliberate practice. Modern psychology labels this principle "exposure," but the concept is ancient. Stoic philosophers, through the practice of *premeditatio malorum*—the premeditation of adversity—recognised that rehearsing potential difficulties inoculates the mind against shock. Whereas avoidance strengthens the link between discomfort and danger, exposure weakens it, replacing reflexive fear with informed familiarity. The aim is not reckless immersion, but structured engagement with discomfort in doses that are challenging yet survivable. This chapter's central insight is that discomfort need not be an enemy to be outmanoeuvred; it is a stimulus to be trained for.

Micro-exposure lies at the heart of this approach. Large, dramatic confrontations with fear are rarely necessary—and can, in fact, backfire—overwhelming the nervous system and reinforcing avoidance. Instead, small, repeatable exposures recalibrate the brain's threat detection system gradually. A salesperson fearful of rejection does not begin by cold-calling a hundred strangers; rather, they start with brief, low-stakes interactions—a greeting to a stranger in a café, a short conversation with a colleague they tend to avoid.

Each micro-exposure functions as both behavioural and neurological feedback: "This sensation is tolerable; I can function despite it." Over time, the body stops triggering alarms at the first flicker of discomfort.

Tolerance training extends equally to the body's internal signals. Anxiety is often treated as a purely cognitive phenomenon, yet its grip is as physiological as it is mental. Accelerated heart rate, shallow breathing, muscle tension, shifts in sensory perception—all contribute to the sense of alarm. Misinterpreted, these signals create a feedback loop: sensations trigger fear, fear amplifies sensations, and the spiral continues. Body calibration drills interrupt this loop. Breath pacing stabilises the nervous system under duress; posture resets the brain's appraisal of safety; sensory grounding anchors attention in the present rather than catastrophic projections. These are practical, evidence-aligned interventions, informed by both ancient philosophy and contemporary neuroscience, giving tangible leverage over the body even when the mind is unsettled.

Discomfort tolerance cannot be built theoretically; it is learned experientially. Anxiety thrives on overestimation: imagined discomfort feels sharper and more enduring than reality proves. The only remedy is direct measurement. By noting the intensity of sensations before, during, and after exposure, and comparing prediction with outcome, we recalibrate our internal models. Often, what was feared as intolerable is revealed as temporary, fluctuating, and manageable. Repeated experience erodes catastrophic bias, replacing imagined catastrophe with lived evidence of endurance.

The contemporary world makes this training more urgent. Constant connectivity exposes us to public scrutiny—online criticism, visible performance metrics, the sense of being permanently "on." A culture that praises composure under pressure yet punishes self-protective avoidance rewards precisely the skills that discomfort tolerance develops: emotional stamina, physical poise, cognitive clarity. In this sense, practising discomfort is not merely a mental health strategy; it is a competitive advantage in any field that prizes composure under observation.

This chapter does not catalogue discomforts to be pursued for their own sake; it presents a practical framework for expanding functional capacity. It begins by dismantling the false logic of avoidance, then introduces structured micro-exposure to rewire thought and physiology. From there, you will learn to work with bodily signals, not against them, employing calibration drills to maintain control under pressure. Finally, the chapter addresses the crucial step of measuring experience to counter distorted expectations. The result is a shift from defensive living—constantly scanning for threats and evading them—to active engagement, confident that discomfort can be faced without being consumed.

The principle is deceptively simple: the more you practise being uncomfortable, the less power discomfort holds over you. This is not ascetic self-denial nor empty bravado; it is strategic conditioning. Soldiers train under stress not for enjoyment, but to transform unknown threat into familiar challenge. Athletes push through strain to render extraordinary effort routine. You will apply the same principle—not on battlefields or in stadiums, but in the arenas of everyday life where anxiety once dictated the rules. Through consistent, deliberate practice, discomfort will cease to signal retreat and instead mark an opportunity to act, a cue that growth and progress await.

Why Avoidance Feels Logical—But Isn't

Avoidance is one of the most deceptively persuasive strategies the human mind ever devised. On the surface, it offers the neatest of solutions: if something triggers anxiety, remove yourself from it, and the anxiety fades. Your body calms, your thoughts settle, and the immediate threat—whether real or imagined—seems to recede. The feedback loop appears to prove its own wisdom. What is less obvious, and vastly more dangerous, is that every time avoidance is rewarded with relief, it deepens the brain's conviction that the avoided situation is dangerous and that withdrawal was the only safe option. *This is the central paradox: the more we avoid, the more fragile we become.*

The logic of avoidance is appealing because it mimics effective risk management. In everyday life, steering clear of genuine hazards is an adaptive behaviour; no one would question the prudence of avoiding a collapsing building or a venomous snake. The problem is that anxiety disorders—and even everyday chronic worry—convince us to treat discomfort itself as a hazard. The trigger may be giving a presentation, boarding a plane, attending a social gathering, or even experiencing a racing heartbeat. In these cases, avoidance does not protect us from actual danger; it shields us from an internal state we fear we cannot handle. That protection is temporary, but the cost is permanent: we outsource our confidence to circumstances, making our stability conditional on keeping our lives free from certain experiences.

Behavioural psychology has mapped this process in detail. Avoidance is maintained by what is known as *negative reinforcement*: an action is repeated because it removes an unpleasant stimulus. In the case of anxiety, the unpleasant stimulus is not the situation itself but the physiological arousal—pounding heart, sweaty palms, tightening chest—that the situation evokes. By avoiding, we turn off the alarm, but we also fail to learn that the alarm would have subsided on its own. Over time, the threshold for triggering the alarm lowers; situations that once caused mild discomfort now provoke intense anxiety. In effect, avoidance teaches the brain that fear is intolerable and must be escaped at all costs, eroding tolerance for uncertainty and discomfort.

Consider a common example: someone with a mild fear of public speaking declines an invitation to give a short talk. They feel an immediate rush of relief—no more days of dread leading up to the event, no more rehearsed lines dissolving in their mind. Yet the next time they are asked, the fear spikes even sooner, because their nervous system has learned that speaking is something to be avoided. What's more, their self-image subtly shifts: *I am not someone who can handle that.* The avoidance becomes a self-fulfilling prophecy.

Modern research confirms that avoidance not only sustains anxiety but broadens its scope. A person who avoids driving on motorways after one panic episode may soon begin to avoid long-distance travel altogether. Someone who skips social events due to anxiety about being judged may start withdrawing from professional opportunities. The protective walls built to keep distress out also keep life out. This narrowing of lived experience is often so gradual that people fail to notice the cumulative loss until it is profound—relationships weakened, ambitions sidelined, everyday autonomy diminished.

Part of avoidance's seductive power lies in its framing as a rational choice. We tell ourselves that we are "just not in the mood," that we will face the situation "when we feel ready," or that it is "not worth the stress." These explanations soothe the cognitive dissonance between wanting a richer life and retreating from it. But readiness rarely arrives on its own; without exposure, the nervous system has no opportunity to recalibrate. This is why avoidance masquerading as self-care is particularly insidious—it can feel like wisdom while quietly teaching helplessness.

It is important to distinguish avoidance from strategic rest or boundary-setting. Choosing not to engage in certain situations for the sake of alignment with your values is different from ducking them out of fear. The difference lies in whether the decision expands or contracts your capacity for life. Avoidance contracts it, because it is not about choosing the best option but about eliminating the one you fear, regardless of potential benefits. The guiding question here is stark: *If I knew I could handle the discomfort, would I choose differently?* If the answer is yes, avoidance is in play.

From a Stoic perspective, avoidance undermines the very skill needed to live well: the ability to distinguish between what we can and cannot control, and to act accordingly. By fleeing from discomfort, we implicitly try to control the uncontrollable—namely, the fact that life will present us with unpredictable challenges. Epictetus warned that it is not events themselves that disturb us, but our judgements about them. Avoidance entrenches the judgement that certain experiences are unbearable, ensuring that they will remain so. The more one retreats from these encounters, the more alien they become, and the harder it is to meet them with equanimity when they inevitably arise.

Neuroscience provides a parallel view. The amygdala, a brain structure central to threat detection, learns through experience. If we confront a feared stimulus and nothing catastrophic happens, the amygdala's future response is tempered. If we avoid the stimulus, the amygdala never receives corrective feedback, and the fear response remains at full intensity. Worse, avoidance can generalise: the brain begins to associate not just the specific trigger but related contexts with danger. This is why avoiding one social event can make the idea of socialising in general more daunting, or avoiding one type of physical exertion due to anxiety about heart rate can make all exercise feel threatening.

The long-term costs of avoidance are not merely emotional; they are behavioural and even physiological. Muscles kept idle lose strength; skills left unused degrade; networks untended dissolve. The same is true for the mind. Discomfort tolerance atrophies without regular use, and the anxiety threshold drops until even small challenges feel overwhelming. Life becomes a project in minimisation rather than expansion, guided less by what is meaningful and more by what is least triggering. This is not the avoidance of danger—it is the avoidance of living.

Breaking the cycle requires recognising avoidance for what it is: a short-term comfort that robs long-term freedom. The first step is catching the moment of decision, when the mind generates a plausible-sounding excuse to step back. These are often rehearsed scripts—*it's too much right now, I'll do it later, this isn't important*—that deserve interrogation. The second step is to consider the actual cost of avoidance in terms of lost opportunities, diminished self-trust, and reinforced fear. This is not about shaming oneself for retreat, but about making the invisible ledger of avoidance visible.

What follows is not a call to reckless confrontation, but to deliberate, measured engagement with the situations avoidance has begun to dictate. The antidote to avoidance is not mere willpower but a structured process of reclaiming agency: testing feared scenarios in small doses, recalibrating bodily responses, and building an evidence base that discomfort is survivable. The relief that comes from avoidance is fleeting and brittle; the confidence that comes from facing discomfort is durable and transferable. One shrinks your world, the other expands it. The logic of avoidance may feel convincing, but the longer view reveals its bankruptcy. It offers safety at the expense of strength—a trade no one makes consciously, yet one that, unexamined, defines the boundaries of a life.

The Role of Micro-Exposure

The human nervous system is not designed to grow stronger by avoiding stress—it adapts by meeting it in manageable doses. This is as true for emotional and psychological resilience as it is for physical fitness. Yet when it comes to anxiety, most people attempt the equivalent of staying off the playing field entirely, hoping confidence will return on its own. It rarely does. The paradox is that *the only reliable way to reduce the power of a feared experience is to engage with it*, but in a way that does not overwhelm. This is where micro-exposure comes in: the practice of facing discomfort in deliberately small, tolerable increments that allow the mind and body to re-learn safety without triggering full-blown distress.

The ancient Stoics understood this principle in philosophical rather than clinical terms. Their practice of *premeditatio malorum*—the premeditation of evils—involved mentally rehearsing possible hardships before they occurred. Marcus Aurelius would imagine encountering insult, betrayal, illness, or sudden loss, not as a form of pessimism, but as a mental vaccine against shock and panic. The aim was not to dwell on catastrophe, but to shrink its power by becoming familiar with its outlines in advance. In modern therapeutic terms, *premeditatio malorum* is a form of cognitive exposure: it helps the mind recognise that the thought of adversity need not trigger avoidance, and that preparing for difficulty reduces the emotional spike when it arrives.

Micro-exposure takes this Stoic insight and translates it into behavioural training. The method begins with identifying a specific trigger—say, social anxiety in meetings—and designing the smallest possible step toward it that still creates mild discomfort. This might mean attending a meeting without speaking, or speaking only once to ask a clarifying question. The point is not to force heroic leaps but to build a sequence of experiences where each step feels challenging yet manageable. As with physical training, progress comes from gradual increases in difficulty, not from attempting the equivalent of lifting double your capacity on day one.

The neuroscience behind micro-exposure is well-established. The amygdala, which plays a central role in fear conditioning, requires repeated, safe encounters with a feared stimulus to recalibrate. Each exposure provides "disconfirming evidence" to the brain: *I felt anxiety, but nothing catastrophic happened.* Over time, the brain updates its threat model, reducing the intensity of the fear response. Skipping these exposures by avoiding the trigger denies the nervous system this learning opportunity.

The advantage of micro-exposure over more aggressive confrontation methods is that it reduces the likelihood of a "flooding" experience—an encounter so overwhelming that it reinforces the belief that the trigger is unmanageable. Flooding may work for some, but for many it leads to setback and renewed avoidance. Micro-exposure, by contrast, creates a steady stream of small victories. These accumulate into a broader sense of competence: if you can handle a minor version of the fear, you can handle a slightly larger one, and so on. *It is the consistency, not the intensity, of exposure that rewires fear.*

Modern life presents opportunities for micro-exposure that go far beyond clinical settings. Someone who fears public speaking might begin by recording themselves talking for thirty seconds and playing it back, then gradually increase both the duration and the presence of a live audience—perhaps a trusted friend, then a small team, then a larger group. A person who fears flying could start by watching videos of take-offs and landings, then visiting an airport without boarding, then taking a short flight with a trusted companion. The sequence is always personalised, and the pace is determined not by arbitrary deadlines but by the individual's ability to meet each stage without spiralling into panic.

Linking this to *premeditatio malorum* enriches the process. Before each micro-exposure, the Stoics would recommend a deliberate mental preparation: briefly picturing what could go wrong, and rehearsing the calm acceptance you would bring to it. If you fear being judged while speaking up in a meeting, you might imagine someone reacting with indifference or mild criticism—and then imagine yourself responding without collapse or defensiveness. This mental preview inoculates against the element of surprise, one of the main amplifiers of anxiety. By combining imagined adversity with real-world micro-exposures, you address both the cognitive and physiological components of fear.

Critically, micro-exposure is not simply about enduring discomfort—it is about active learning. After each step, reflection is key. What actually happened? How did your body react? What did you predict beforehand, and how did reality compare? This post-exposure debrief transforms the experience from mere tolerance into evidence gathering. Over time, the evidence tends to converge on a pattern: *the feared outcome is rare, and the discomfort fades faster than expected.* This is the kind of data that permanently alters the fear circuitry.

One of the most common objections to micro-exposure is that it feels artificial, contrived, or even indulgent compared to the "real" challenges life throws at us. But this misses the point. The aim is to train the nervous system in controlled conditions so that when genuine, high-stakes challenges arise, the system is already familiar with discomfort and less likely to overreact. A Stoic would remind us that you would not wait until a storm to learn how to sail—you would practise in calmer waters first, increasing difficulty as your skill grows.

A further strength of micro-exposure is that it aligns with the broader Stoic ethic of living according to nature. Humans are adaptive creatures; our nervous systems are built to learn from repeated, safe engagement with our environment. Avoidance short-circuits that process, creating a mismatch between the actual demands of life and our perceived capacity to meet them. Micro-exposure restores this alignment, teaching us to meet challenges with proportionate—not exaggerated—responses.

The cultural pace of the present day makes this approach more necessary than ever. Constant connectivity and performance pressure can amplify the temptation to avoid situations that might reveal imperfection or invite discomfort. Micro-exposure, combined with the mental discipline of *premeditatio malorum*, offers a counterweight: a deliberate, structured method for expanding rather than contracting your range of action. It reframes discomfort not as a signal to retreat, but as a signal to practise, in small, calculated doses, until mastery emerges.

The endgame of micro-exposure is not fearlessness in the naïve sense, but confidence in your ability to act despite fear. By incrementally dismantling avoidance patterns and rehearsing the calm acceptance of possible setbacks, you transform anxiety triggers from looming threats into manageable tasks. In doing so, you not only weaken the grip of specific fears but strengthen the overall capacity to navigate uncertainty—arguably the most valuable skill in both Stoic philosophy and modern life.

Body Calibration Drills

The body does not simply reflect anxiety—it participates in it. A rapid heartbeat, shallow breathing, tight shoulders, a narrowed field of vision: these are not just symptoms but amplifiers of fear. Left unchecked, they create a feedback loop in which physical sensations are misread as evidence of imminent danger, pushing the mind into overdrive. To interrupt this cycle, it is not enough to reason with anxious thoughts; you must engage the body directly. *Body calibration* is the practice of using targeted physical interventions to reassert control over your state, teaching your nervous system that it can downshift from threat mode even when discomfort is present.

Breath pacing is the most accessible and immediate of these interventions. Anxiety is often accompanied by rapid, irregular breathing driven by the sympathetic nervous system. This pattern signals to the brain that you are in danger, even when no external threat exists. Reversing this requires intentional control of the respiratory rhythm—breathing in through the nose for a count of four, pausing for a brief moment, and exhaling through the mouth for a count of six to eight. The extended exhalation activates the parasympathetic "rest and digest" branch of the autonomic nervous system, sending a physiological message that conditions are safe enough to stand down. The effect is not merely psychological; measurable changes occur in heart rate variability, a key indicator of stress resilience. Crucially, *the goal is not to eliminate anxiety instantly, but to keep your physiology within a workable range* so that panic does not take over decision-making.

Posture resets address another often-overlooked contributor to anxiety spirals. When threatened, humans instinctively adopt a defensive posture: hunched shoulders, lowered head, inward rotation of the arms. While adaptive in moments of genuine danger, this stance reinforces a perception of vulnerability when it becomes habitual. Adopting an open, upright posture—shoulders back, chest lifted, feet grounded—can subtly but powerfully alter your emotional stance. Research in embodied cognition has shown that posture not only reflects mood but can influence it, modulating levels of confidence, perceived threat, and readiness to act. A posture reset during an anxiety surge is not a superficial "power pose" exercise; it is a recalibration of the body's threat signals, allowing the mind to reframe the situation from a position of capability rather than collapse.

Sensory grounding is the third core drill, designed to interrupt the runaway chain of anxious thoughts by anchoring awareness in the present moment through physical sensation. This is not a vague call to "be mindful," but a structured, active process. You might press your feet firmly into the ground, notice the texture of the surface beneath you, and feel the weight distribution shift as you gently sway. Or you might hold an object—a pen, a cold drink, a smooth stone—and attend to its temperature, texture, and weight. These signals compete with and dilute the dominance of catastrophic mental imagery, giving your cognitive system a foothold from which to reassert control. Importantly, sensory grounding works best when the cues are neutral or slightly pleasant, rather than emotionally loaded.

What unites breath pacing, posture resets, and sensory grounding is that they are *trainable skills*, not emergency improvisations. Waiting until the peak of an anxiety surge to try them for the first time is like attempting a complicated dance move in the middle of a live performance without rehearsal. The drills become most effective when practised in calm or mildly stressed states so that they are second nature when genuinely needed. This is the principle of state-dependent learning: skills rehearsed in a range of emotional states are more readily retrievable under similar conditions in the future.

A practical example illustrates the integration of these drills. Imagine you are about to give an unplanned presentation in a meeting—an event that reliably spikes your anxiety. Your breath has quickened, your shoulders are tight, and your mind is racing through possible missteps. The first move is breath pacing: you silently anchor yourself with a slow inhale, a brief pause, and a longer exhale. As you do this twice more, you consciously lift your chest and roll your shoulders back, occupying a posture that makes your diaphragm's movement easier and signals physical readiness. You then discreetly press your feet into the floor, noticing the firmness beneath them, the pressure points shifting slightly as you adjust your stance. Within a minute, you have moved your body out of the narrow, threat-dominated stance and into one that supports composure and functional thinking.

From a Stoic perspective, these drills embody the principle that while external events are often beyond our control, our internal responses can be trained. Marcus Aurelius wrote of "standing firm like a rock" against the crashing waves of circumstance. Breath pacing steadies the internal tides, posture resets align the body with the mind's intended course, and sensory grounding roots you in the moment rather than in the swirl of imagined futures. This is not mystical resilience—it is mechanical, physiological, and repeatable.

Critics sometimes dismiss body-based techniques as superficial, arguing that they address only the surface manifestations of anxiety rather than its deeper causes. This misses a key truth: the surface and the depth are connected. Calming the body does not solve every problem, but it buys the mental bandwidth to address them without the distortions of panic. It shifts you from survival mode to problem-solving mode. By repeatedly demonstrating that you can influence your state through physical calibration, you weaken the learned helplessness that fuels chronic anxiety.

In high-performance fields—aviation, surgery, competitive sport—these drills are standard, not optional. Pilots rehearse breathing protocols to prevent hypoxia-induced panic; surgeons consciously adjust posture to maintain precision under fatigue; athletes use grounding techniques between plays to reset focus. The same physiology is at play in everyday anxiety triggers. Adopting these methods is not about over-dramatising ordinary stressors, but about borrowing proven tools from contexts where performance under pressure is non-negotiable.

Ultimately, body calibration drills do more than ride out anxiety surges—they retrain the relationship between bodily sensation and mental interpretation. Over time, rapid heartbeat, tense muscles, or heightened alertness cease to be automatic danger signals; they become recognised as manageable fluctuations in a responsive system. This is the essence of riding the wave rather than being submerged by it: not fighting the body's reactions, but guiding them toward stability with practiced, deliberate action. By integrating breath pacing, posture resets, and sensory grounding into daily life, you turn moments of physiological turbulence into opportunities for mastery, reinforcing the knowledge that composure is not the absence of stress, but the ability to steer through it.

Data Over Drama

Anxiety is rarely an honest reporter. It exaggerates, speculates, and often makes predictions that would shame even the most sensationalist tabloid. Left unchecked, this mental habit turns everyday challenges into imagined catastrophes, convincing you that discomfort will be unbearable and the outcome intolerable. Yet when the event passes, the actual experience is often markedly less severe than the forecasted one. The problem is that without a deliberate process to compare prediction with reality, the mind retains its distorted forecast as truth. *Data over drama* is the antidote—a disciplined practice of tracking, measuring, and confronting the gap between what you feared and what actually occurred.

Consider a common scenario: a professional dreads delivering a short update in a meeting, convinced their voice will shake, their mind will go blank, and colleagues will silently judge them. In the moment, the discomfort is real—heart racing, palms sweating—but the feared disaster rarely materialises. They manage to speak clearly enough, no one seems hostile, and the meeting moves on. Yet because there is no conscious recording of this discrepancy between fear and reality, the next time the same situation arises, the mind runs the same inflated forecast. Without evidence to counter the drama, the cycle remains unbroken.

Tracking actual versus predicted discomfort forces an encounter with the truth. This can be done with a simple two-column record: before an event, rate the expected intensity of discomfort on a scale of 0 to 10, along with the predicted worst-case outcomes. After the event, rate the actual intensity and note the outcomes that occurred. Over time, a pattern emerges—predictions are almost always more severe than reality, and the worst-case scenarios almost never play out. The act of collecting this data is not just clerical; it changes the relationship between you and your anxiety. Fear thrives in vagueness, but it weakens when confronted with clear, empirical patterns.

The method also clarifies an important Stoic principle: that most suffering lies not in the event itself but in the anticipation of it. Epictetus reminded his students that we are disturbed not by things, but by the views we take of them. By quantifying those views, you create a feedback loop that recalibrates your threat estimation system. The goal is not to deny discomfort—it is to scale it accurately. This shift from narrative to evidence transforms anxiety from an untouchable force into a measurable, influenceable process.

One of the key benefits of the *data over drama* approach is its ability to challenge what behavioural scientists call "affective forecasting errors"—the human tendency to overestimate both the intensity and duration of future emotional states. People believe that an awkward conversation will haunt them for days, when in fact the emotional residue may fade within minutes. By logging these predictions and outcomes, you create a personal dataset that steadily dismantles the mind's overconfidence in its own dramatic forecasts.

The technique is equally valuable for those whose anxiety manifests physically. For example, a person may fear that jogging in public will lead to overwhelming breathlessness, chest tightness, or even fainting. By noting predicted discomfort levels before the run and actual sensations during and after, they begin to see the discrepancy. The predicted "8 out of 10" distress might turn out to be a "4" and entirely manageable. This lived evidence is far more persuasive to the nervous system than abstract reassurance.

Crucially, *data over drama* is not about minimising or dismissing real challenges. Sometimes the actual discomfort does match or even exceed the prediction. The value in those moments lies in clarity: knowing that the fear was accurate in that case allows you to prepare differently next time, rather than either blindly avoiding the situation or approaching it with false confidence. The practice does not promise comfort; it promises accuracy, and accuracy is what allows for intelligent strategy.

The modern environment makes this method more urgent. In a performance-driven culture where people are evaluated in real time—through metrics, public reviews, and social media visibility—the mind is primed to overestimate social and professional risks. The predicted cost of a misstep becomes inflated far beyond its actual impact. Without systematic correction, you live in permanent anticipation of an imagined fallout that rarely occurs. Recording real outcomes is a quiet rebellion against this cultural pressure, a way of reclaiming agency from the collective drama.

In high-stakes professions, variants of this approach are already embedded in training. Emergency responders review bodycam footage against their anticipatory notes to refine decision-making under pressure. Athletes log expected versus actual fatigue during events to adjust pacing strategies. Pilots compare simulator anxiety ratings with in-flight performance to recalibrate their threat perception. These are not rituals of self-congratulation but tools of precision—recognising where the mind misreads reality and updating the internal map accordingly.

Implementing the practice in daily life can be done with minimal friction. A small notebook, a spreadsheet, or a note-taking app can serve as the tracking tool. The key is consistency: every time you face a situation you anticipate with anxiety—whether it's a conversation, a public appearance, or an unfamiliar task—you log both the forecast and the reality. Over weeks and months, your brain is presented with undeniable evidence: the story it told was not the story that unfolded. This cumulative evidence has a desensitising effect, shrinking the drama's influence over your behaviour.

There is a philosophical elegance to this process. In replacing emotional speculation with measured observation, you are enacting the Stoic discipline of assent—refusing to give automatic agreement to the first, most dramatic impression. You become a curator of your own internal newsfeed, fact-checking every alarming headline your mind runs. This is the opposite of blind optimism; it is a rigorously informed realism. And from realism, confidence grows—not the brittle confidence of ignoring risk, but the grounded confidence of seeing it clearly.

Over time, the practice creates a noticeable shift in day-to-day decision-making. You no longer waste as much mental energy rehearsing unlikely disasters, because your own data shows how seldom they occur. Discomfort stops being an automatic stop sign and becomes something you can navigate with increasing skill. The drama still tries to speak, but it has lost its monopoly on the truth. You have built an evidence base that says otherwise—and the more you use it, the more accurate your fear responses become.

Chapter 4
The Values Compass

In moments of acute stress, we tend to believe our actions are driven by logic or sheer urgency. Yet beneath the visible surface of choices lies a subtler, far more enduring force: values. Whether acknowledged or not, these act as an internal compass, shaping not just what we do, but how we judge ourselves afterwards. Anxiety, however, has a way of clouding this compass. The mind narrows, prioritising immediate comfort over long-term significance, and what truly matters recedes into the background. Such concessions may seem trivial in isolation, but repeated over time, they erode confidence, leaving a person unmoored from both purpose and identity. To act decisively amid fear, one must first render the invisible tangible—articulating the principles that will guide action when panic threatens to dominate.

Values are neither slogans nor mere preferences. They are the standards you hold as non-negotiable, even when upholding them incurs cost or discomfort. In high-stakes moments—whether a doctor deliberating whether to challenge a questionable treatment, or a parent enforcing a difficult boundary—clear values provide a framework that resists the instinct to capitulate to fear. Fear does not vanish; rather, it loses its monopoly over the decision. Anchored in values, anxiety becomes an early-warning system, signalling that what lies ahead touches identity and purpose.

Modern life constantly confronts us with collisions between comfort and principle. The easy option—avoiding risk, conflict, or exposure—presents itself as rational, reinforced by a culture obsessed with speed, convenience, and the minimisation of discomfort. Yet the harder right—the choice aligned with our deepest sense of integrity—rarely comes with a fanfare. It often feels, in the moment, like stepping into a storm: applying for a role you dread failing at, acknowledging a professional mistake, confronting a friend's unethical remark. The outcomes cannot be precisely predicted, but the satisfaction of acting in accordance with principle endures. Without a deliberate method to define and hold to such values, these opportunities slip by, lost to hesitation.

Defining values is not an exercise in abstract idealism; it is a practical necessity under pressure. The Stoics recognised this clearly. Marcus Aurelius understood living according to nature as aligning each act with virtue—justice, courage, self-discipline, wisdom—rather than with fleeting moods or external rewards. In modern terms, this means determining, outside crises, which principles will serve as fixed coordinates when stress distorts perception. This clarity acts as an anchor, keeping decisions aligned even when anxiety rises.

Values only reveal their true strength when tested—when upholding them is inconvenient, uncomfortable, or risky. The most reliable litmus test is simple: are you willing to endure discomfort to honour this principle? If not, it is a preference, not a value. This distinction matters because under duress, preferences vanish, but core values endure. The challenge lies in remembering them when the nervous system is overactive, which is why rehearsal is essential. Small, daily choices made in alignment with values build the neural and emotional pathways that support consistency under pressure.

There is a further subtlety: identifying values alone does not guarantee behaviour in accordance with them. Under stress, the brain prioritises immediate harm reduction over long-term alignment. Structured reflection becomes indispensable here. A brief end-of-day review—asking "Did my actions today reflect my values?"—can illuminate where anxiety has diverted decisions. This is not self-criticism but gentle course correction, like a navigator adjusting for drift. Repeated over time, this practice deepens self-awareness, strengthens consistency, and diminishes the regret that follows fear-driven choices.

The promise of a values compass is not that fear vanishes or uncertainty disappears. Rather, it is that decisions acquire a new weight—grounded not in fleeting comfort or avoidance, but in deliberate commitments that define your best self. In a culture that prizes speed and superficial gains, this is quiet resistance: choosing depth over ease, meaning over expedience. Over the long term, these are the choices that lessen anxiety's sway and cultivate the self-respect no short-term comfort could ever provide.

Defining Worthy Action

When pressure rises, most people believe they are acting on logic, instinct, or experience. In reality, much of what drives human behaviour under stress is an unexamined hierarchy of values—an internal ranking of what matters most in the moment. Sometimes these values are clear and consciously chosen; more often, they are inherited from habit, culture, or convenience. The result is that when anxiety strikes, the brain defaults to what feels immediately safe rather than what is ultimately right. Without a deliberate definition of *worthy action*, decisions risk being shaped more by the avoidance of discomfort than by alignment with principle. The cost of that pattern is rarely obvious in a single event. It emerges over time, in the erosion of self-respect, the dulling of ambition, and the quiet accumulation of regrets that could have been prevented by acting with clarity in the first place.

Worthy action is not merely about doing the ethical thing; it is about doing the thing that maintains your alignment with your core identity when the stakes are high. This distinction matters because people often confuse values with preferences. A preference is something you would *like* to honour if circumstances are favourable. A value is something you will honour even when doing so is inconvenient, uncomfortable, or risky. The most revealing test is to ask: *Am I willing to take a personal cost to uphold this?* If the answer is yes, you have identified a value worth using as a guide. In high-stakes situations, this commitment creates a counterweight to fear, giving you an internal reference point that remains stable when emotions fluctuate.

The stress response in the human body was designed for survival, not for moral deliberation. Under threat, the nervous system primes us for speed, narrowing attention to immediate hazards and shortcuts for safety. In evolutionary terms, this served us well—hesitating over whether to confront a predator could be fatal. In modern environments, however, most threats are not physical but psychological: social rejection, career risk, reputational damage. These dangers trigger the same physiological arousal, yet the "fast" decision that avoids immediate discomfort is often the one that undermines our deeper goals. For example, a manager might avoid giving honest feedback to a struggling employee because they fear conflict, despite knowing that clear communication is a stated value for both themselves and their organisation. In the moment, this feels logical; in retrospect, it reveals a drift from principle.

Defining worthy action therefore begins long before the stressful moment arrives. It requires the discipline of identifying values in calm conditions, away from the noise of urgency. This is not an abstract philosophical exercise—it is a practical safeguard. When values are named, articulated, and revisited regularly, they create a mental framework that can be recalled under stress without hesitation. A doctor who has made a personal commitment to "patient safety above institutional convenience" is far more likely to challenge a flawed hospital protocol, even when doing so risks their standing. Without that pre-set compass, the same doctor might default to silence, rationalising that the conflict could harm their career.

However, clarity about values is not enough. Worthy action demands prioritisation, because real-world scenarios often involve competing values. Consider the whistle-blower who must choose between loyalty to colleagues and transparency to the public. Both values may be legitimate, but the decision lies in recognising which value takes precedence in the specific context. This is where the Stoic perspective offers guidance: the ancients held that virtue was indivisible, but its expression required wisdom—phronesis—in balancing justice, courage, and prudence. In modern terms, worthy action is not about blindly following a single value at all costs; it is about discerning which values most require protection in the moment, and accepting the cost of that choice without self-deception.

The process of defining worthy action also involves clarifying the *non-values*—those ideals we may admire in others but do not truly live by ourselves. This is not hypocrisy; it is honest self-knowledge. For example, a person might believe environmental activism is important, but if they are not willing to endure sustained inconvenience for the cause, it is not a core value for them. Recognising this prevents the moral confusion that comes from claiming a value one does not act upon. This honesty is not a lowering of standards but a clearing of false signals that could mislead decision-making under stress.

Case studies reveal that the absence of clearly defined values often manifests not in dramatic moral failure, but in subtle self-betrayal. An academic who values intellectual rigour might nonetheless publish a rushed paper to meet a grant deadline, knowing it lacks the depth they demand of others. A lawyer who values justice might accept a settlement that undermines their client's long-term interests simply to avoid a trial's uncertainty. These actions may bring short-term relief, but they carry a private cost—the quiet knowledge that one acted beneath one's own standards. Over time, repeated compromises normalise the behaviour, making it harder to recognise when a line has been crossed.

Defining worthy action is, therefore, an act of self-defence against the incremental erosion of character. It also reshapes how anxiety is interpreted. Instead of viewing fear as a stop sign, a values-driven perspective treats fear as an indicator of significance: *this matters to me; my identity is involved here*. This reframing shifts the role of anxiety from a paralysing force to a navigational signal. The question becomes not "How do I make the fear go away?" but "Which of my values is this fear protecting, and how do I act in its service?" That shift can turn avoidance into engagement, even when the body is urging retreat.

The discipline of worthy action does not guarantee comfort, but it does deliver clarity. And clarity is what preserves coherence under pressure. In professional environments, leaders who act consistently with their values—even when those actions carry personal cost—tend to inspire trust, attract long-term allies, and leave fewer open ethical wounds in their wake. In personal life, individuals who make decisions in alignment with their values report less regret, even when outcomes are unfavourable, because the choice itself was self-congruent. The opposite pattern—acting out of fear, expedience, or social pressure—may yield temporary safety but often leaves a residue of self-doubt that accumulates with each unworthy compromise.

Worthy action, then, is not a lofty abstraction but a form of strategic resilience. It is a conscious alignment of decision-making with deliberately chosen values, maintained even under the strain of stress. To achieve it requires the preparatory work of naming, testing, and prioritising values, as well as the courage to accept the costs of living by them. This is the architecture that enables a person to navigate not only the external challenges of a volatile world but the internal turbulence of their own fear responses, emerging not unscathed, but unbroken.

From Fear to Function

The presence of anxiety is often treated as evidence of a problem to be eliminated, a signal that something has gone wrong either in the environment or within the individual. Yet this interpretation—while culturally reinforced—is both incomplete and strategically limiting. Anxiety is not solely a malfunction of the nervous system; it is an evolved mechanism designed to highlight situations of potential significance. When reframed with precision, fear can become a prompt to move towards value-driven action rather than an instruction to withdraw. The pivot from avoidance to engagement begins with rejecting the binary view that anxiety is inherently an enemy. Instead, it can be treated as a sophisticated—if sometimes overzealous—messenger that points toward what matters.

Biologically, the anxiety response is a mobilisation system. It elevates heart rate, sharpens sensory processing, and redirects energy to essential functions. These changes are not randomly triggered; they are the body's preparatory measures for confronting challenges that might impact survival or well-being. The flaw in modern contexts is that the same physiological machinery reacts to symbolic threats—uncertain social interactions, career opportunities, financial decisions—with an intensity disproportionate to the actual risk. The instinctive move is to quiet the system by avoiding the triggering situation. This works in the short term but carries a hidden price: each avoidance reinforces the association between the situation and danger, ensuring that anxiety returns stronger the next time. This is the self-reinforcing loop that keeps people trapped.

When values are clearly identified, they offer a crucial counterweight to this loop. A person who holds "integrity in communication" as a core value can reinterpret the dread before a difficult conversation not as a sign to cancel the meeting, but as evidence that the conversation matters enough to provoke fear. The nervous system is doing its job by mobilising resources; the individual's job is to apply those resources in service of the value. The fear becomes directional—a compass pointing towards significance—rather than a stop sign. *The most productive stance is not to wait for fear to subside, but to move with it towards meaningful action.*

This reframing has precedent in Stoic thought. The practice of premeditatio malorum, in which one deliberately contemplates possible misfortunes, was not designed to cultivate pessimism but to train the mind to remain anchored in principle despite imagined adversity. By envisioning feared scenarios in advance, the Stoics weakened the reflexive urge to avoid discomfort. Modern behavioural science converges on a similar insight: exposure to feared stimuli, when done gradually and with intention, leads to desensitisation. The crucial distinction here is the motivation behind exposure. When undertaken simply to "get over" fear, exposure can feel like an endurance test. When undertaken to act in alignment with one's values, the same exposure gains meaning and becomes more sustainable.

Consider the example of a medical trainee who feels paralysed at the prospect of performing a first unsupervised procedure. The anxiety is acute, the physiological markers unmistakable—sweaty palms, shallow breathing, racing heart. Avoidance is easy to justify: patient safety could be compromised, self-confidence could be damaged. Yet if the trainee's core value is "commitment to patient care through competence," then the fear signals not a reason to step back, but the presence of a critical growth moment. Performing the procedure—under safe supervision—becomes a values-driven choice. The anxiety is still there, but it is no longer an argument for retreat.

This approach requires developing a specific mental habit: pausing in the moment of fear to ask, *What value is at stake here?* This question interrupts the automatic avoidance response and shifts attention from the discomfort itself to the underlying reason the situation matters. If no value is at stake, then avoidance might be rational self-preservation. If a core value is implicated, then the discomfort is the price of acting in alignment with oneself. This is not romanticising fear; it is making it functional.

The practical advantage of this reframing is twofold. First, it prevents chronic narrowing of one's world. Avoidance accumulates like sediment, gradually constricting opportunities and freedoms. People who repeatedly sidestep anxiety-triggering situations often find their lives shrinking, their confidence eroding, and their tolerance for uncertainty diminishing. Second, it transforms the emotional tone of engagement. Approaching a challenge because it aligns with a value feels different from approaching it out of mere obligation or external pressure. This sense of purpose can significantly alter how the nervous system processes the event, sometimes lowering the intensity of the fear itself.

There is also a subtle but important shift in self-perception when fear is treated as a values cue. The narrative changes from "I am someone who suffers from anxiety" to "I am someone who notices anxiety when my values are in play." This reframing protects self-efficacy. Instead of seeing oneself as at the mercy of fear, one sees fear as a normal physiological event that appears when the stakes are high. It becomes a familiar part of the terrain rather than an intruder. Over time, this familiarity reduces secondary anxiety—the fear of fear—which is often more disabling than the original sensation.

Some critics argue that this approach risks overexposure, pushing people into situations where anxiety overwhelms capacity. This is a valid caution, and it underscores the importance of graded engagement. Aligning with values does not mean reckless immersion in the most feared scenario; it means taking the next viable step that honours the value without tipping into panic. The aim is to strengthen the link between values and action, not to break it through overwhelming distress. A public speaker who values "sharing knowledge" might begin by addressing a small, supportive group before progressing to a larger audience, each step guided by the same value but scaled to current capacity.

From a neurological perspective, this approach leverages the brain's capacity for associative learning. By pairing the experience of fear with successful, value-consistent action, the brain learns that anxiety is not a reliable predictor of catastrophe. Instead, it becomes linked with experiences of growth and self-respect. The hippocampus and amygdala, key structures in processing fear and memory, gradually recalibrate their threat assessments. This is how fear transitions from an obstacle to a functional signal—through repeated, intentional experiences where anxiety accompanies, but does not dictate, behaviour.

This shift from fear to function is not instantaneous; it requires deliberate practice. But the alternative—letting fear default to avoidance—guarantees the perpetuation of the anxiety cycle. Each time fear is met with value-driven action, the nervous system's predictive model changes. The mind begins to expect that anxiety will be followed by constructive engagement rather than retreat. Over time, this expectation reshapes both the emotional experience of fear and the range of actions considered possible. The person who once saw anxiety as an enemy begins to see it as a challenging but useful ally, a signpost pointing towards moments that define who they are.

Choosing the Harder Right

The most consequential decisions in life rarely present themselves in a clean contest between good and bad. Far more often, they appear as a tension between what aligns with one's values and what protects one's comfort. The easy path offers immediate relief, the harder one demands effort, risk, and—frequently—exposure to discomfort. In these moments, moral clarity is not simply about recognising what is right; it is about acting on it despite the gravitational pull of convenience, safety, or approval. *Courage is not the absence of fear but the refusal to subordinate principle to comfort.*

The harder right becomes visible in moments when the cost of acting in accordance with one's values is tangible and immediate, while the cost of compromise is abstract and deferred. Take the case of a senior engineer in a technology firm who discovers a flaw in a widely used product. The defect is unlikely to cause harm in the short term, and management pressures her to "let it pass" until the next development cycle to avoid costly delays. Her values—integrity and accountability—demand disclosure and immediate correction. Yet doing so risks her professional standing, invites conflict with leadership, and may even jeopardise her career. The easier choice is to comply quietly, preserving her role and comfort. The harder right is to voice the issue and insist on remediation, knowing it could provoke significant backlash.

What makes such decisions truly difficult is not simply the presence of fear, but the ambiguity surrounding the outcome. Choosing comfort almost always produces a predictable and short-term gain: stress subsides, approval is maintained, and one's position is preserved. Choosing the harder right trades that certainty for the possibility—sometimes slim—of long-term respect, self-alignment, and societal benefit. This asymmetry encourages procrastination, rationalisation, or complete avoidance. The individual convinces themselves that "timing is not right" or "I'll act when I have more security," but each delay corrodes the habit of value-driven action, making the next moment of choice harder still.

It is here that the Stoic perspective offers both challenge and clarity. The Stoics argued that virtue, not comfort, is the sole good, and that the role of discomfort is often to illuminate where virtue lies. Discomfort signals that something significant is at stake, and its presence should invite closer inspection rather than immediate retreat. In modern psychological terms, discomfort is an activation of the threat-response system—often exaggerated, but not meaningless. When examined through the lens of one's core values, it becomes a navigational tool. The question shifts from "How do I avoid this feeling?" to "What does this feeling tell me about what matters here?"

Case histories show that the harder right is rarely about grand heroics; it is about persistent, often unglamorous acts of alignment. A school headteacher faced with the decision to expel a popular but repeatedly disruptive student must weigh the community's demand for leniency against her commitment to creating a safe learning environment for all. Upholding discipline will invite criticism from influential parents and could harm her reputation. Yet compromising on her principles will erode her credibility with staff and students alike. In acting according to her values, she endures the discomfort of conflict, trusting that the integrity of her leadership will, in time, justify the cost.

Interestingly, the difficulty of these choices is magnified in cultures and workplaces that reward short-term harmony over principled dissent. People learn, often unconsciously, that avoiding friction is the surest path to social acceptance. Over time, the nervous system begins to equate the preservation of comfort with survival, treating value-driven dissent as a direct threat. This is why training oneself to choose the harder right is not merely a moral exercise but a physiological one—it involves reconditioning the body to tolerate the discomfort that accompanies principled action.

One practical strategy for building this capacity is to rehearse smaller, lower-stakes acts of choosing discomfort in service of values. This could mean speaking up in a meeting when one has a dissenting but well-founded perspective, even when silence would be easier. It could mean declining an invitation to a lucrative but ethically dubious collaboration. Each instance creates a record in the mind that fear can coexist with—and even energise—meaningful action. Over time, this record becomes a form of embodied confidence: the knowledge that one can survive the social, emotional, and professional consequences of value-based choices.

There is also a subtler, internal dimension to choosing the harder right: resisting the temptation to rewrite one's values to match one's comfort. When faced with a decision that threatens ease or safety, it is tempting to "adjust" the definition of integrity, courage, or fairness so that the easier choice fits within it. This form of self-deception erodes both personal credibility and the trust of others. The most resilient individuals maintain clarity about their values even when it would be psychologically convenient to blur them. They recognise that the discomfort of acting in accordance with principle is temporary, but the self-doubt generated by compromise can linger for years.

History is filled with figures who exemplified the harder right in action—not because they lacked fear, but because they placed their values above it. Whistle-blowers who exposed systemic corruption, activists who endured imprisonment for their cause, scientists who resisted political pressure to falsify data—all demonstrate the same pattern: a willingness to endure short-term loss for long-term fidelity to principle. These examples are instructive not as unattainable ideals but as reminders that the underlying mechanism—valuing integrity over comfort—is available to anyone in any sphere of life.

The recurring thread in all such cases is that the harder right is rarely chosen in a vacuum. It is supported by preparation, by the cultivation of discomfort tolerance, and by a clear articulation of one's core values before the moment of decision arrives. In the heat of conflict, there is little time to construct these from scratch. This is why reflective practices, such as end-of-day value audits or deliberate rehearsal of potential challenges, are so effective: they prime the mind to recognise the harder right when it emerges, reducing the lag between recognition and action.

Ultimately, choosing the harder right is not a single event but a discipline—a way of meeting the inevitable collisions between values and comfort with deliberate alignment. Each time one chooses in favour of values, the act reinforces identity: *this is the kind of person I am.* Over time, that identity becomes a stabilising force, one that can withstand both internal discomfort and external pressure. And while comfort will always tempt, the rewards of alignment—self-respect, credibility, and the quiet confidence of living in accordance with one's own principles—remain unmatched.

Daily Compass Check

In the blur of modern life, days pass quickly but not always consciously. We rush from one demand to the next, attending to deadlines, obligations, and distractions with little time to register whether our actions actually reflect our deeper principles. This drift is not usually the result of malicious intent; it is the natural by-product of a world designed to prioritise urgency over importance. The trouble is that a life lived without frequent realignment to values is one that can deviate far from the course we intended, often without our noticing. *The gap between what we say we value and what we actually do grows in silence, and left unchecked, it can widen into a chasm.* The

Daily Compass Check is a two-minute discipline designed to close that gap before it becomes unbridgeable.

The idea is disarmingly simple: at the end of each day, ask a brief set of focused questions that compare the day's actions against your stated values. This is not about compiling a moral scorecard or rehearsing guilt. It is about recalibration. In the same way that a pilot regularly checks coordinates to ensure the aircraft remains on course, a person seeking to live a values-based life benefits from small, frequent adjustments rather than relying on a dramatic correction after months or years of neglect. The Stoics practised evening reflection precisely for this purpose—Seneca, for example, wrote of examining the entire day in detail, identifying where he had acted well and where he had failed, with the aim of improving tomorrow rather than punishing himself for today.

What makes the Daily Compass Check distinct from traditional self-reflection exercises is its brevity and specificity. Many reflection routines fail because they demand too much time or become sprawling narratives that wander away from actionable insight. Here, the narrow focus is deliberate: *Did my actions today reflect my values? If not, what would I do differently tomorrow in a similar situation?* The economy of the exercise prevents it from being abandoned when fatigue sets in, while its precision keeps it anchored in behavioural reality rather than drifting into vague intentions.

Real-world examples show the power of such micro-reflections. A surgeon who incorporates this practice into her nightly routine may notice that, despite valuing patience and clarity in communication, she snapped at a junior colleague during a stressful operation. Recognising this allows her to prepare a deliberate correction—an apology, perhaps, and a conscious effort to maintain composure in similar circumstances. Without this deliberate check, the incident might dissolve into the fog of memory, never addressed and never improved upon, subtly eroding both her professional relationships and her sense of alignment with her values.

The psychology behind the Daily Compass Check is clear: humans are prone to cognitive dissonance, the discomfort that arises when our actions conflict with our self-image or stated values. Left unexamined, we unconsciously resolve this discomfort not by changing our actions but by adjusting our self-perception or rationalising the behaviour. A nightly check disrupts this process. It brings the dissonance into conscious awareness before the rationalisations harden, making it more likely that behaviour will change to match values rather than the other way around.

The method also counteracts the bias toward emotional memory over factual memory. When we recall a day without structure, we tend to focus on moments of heightened feeling—frustration in traffic, satisfaction at a compliment—rather than on whether our conduct matched our principles. By framing the reflection explicitly around values, we override this tendency, ensuring that the criteria for evaluation are chosen deliberately rather than left to the whims of mood and circumstance.

This discipline does not require the day to have gone well to be valuable. In fact, its greatest benefits often emerge from days filled with missteps. When a business leader, for instance, realises during her reflection that she avoided a difficult conversation because it felt uncomfortable, she has the opportunity to plan an immediate corrective action—perhaps scheduling the discussion for the next day with a clear outline of points to cover. Without that daily prompt, avoidance could easily stretch into weeks, during which time the underlying problem festers.

The two-minute limit serves another important purpose: it prevents over-analysis from mutating into self-recrimination. The goal is to identify, not to indulge in endless rumination. People who are naturally self-critical are particularly prone to turning reflection into a rehearsal of failings. By imposing a strict time boundary, the practice keeps attention on pragmatic adjustment rather than on emotional spiral. This is a values compass, not a confessional booth.

Critically, the Daily Compass Check gains its power from consistency, not from the intensity of any one night's reflection. A single evening of honest assessment may spark a brief burst of corrective action, but when done daily, the practice accumulates into a durable habit of awareness. This is the same principle that underlies physical training: a brief, well-structured workout repeated regularly builds far more strength than an occasional marathon session. Over time, the nightly check conditions the mind to notice value-alignment (or misalignment) in real time, during the day itself, reducing the lag between recognition and course correction.

There is also a social dimension to the practice that should not be overlooked. People who commit to a nightly values check often find themselves more articulate about their principles in conversation, because they are rehearsing their importance daily. This clarity can strengthen relationships, as others come to recognise the consistency between the individual's words and actions. In leadership contexts, the effect is magnified: when a leader demonstrates this internal accountability, it sets a standard for the team, fostering a culture where alignment to shared values is not just aspirational but actively monitored.

The elegance of the Daily Compass Check lies in its adaptability. It can be done silently in one's head, written in a journal, or spoken aloud to a trusted partner. The format matters less than the fidelity to the two central questions and the commitment to consistency. Over time, many practitioners refine their own micro-questions—perhaps adding a prompt about gratitude, or noting one specific moment they are proud of—but these should remain secondary to the central focus on values alignment.

Ultimately, this practice is a guardrail against drift. It is a reminder that values are not abstract statements to be revisited only when life is calm, but active criteria for decision-making, even—especially—when life is demanding. In a world that constantly pulls attention outward, the Daily Compass Check is a way of turning it inward with purpose, ensuring that tomorrow's actions are just a little closer to the life we claim to want. Two minutes may not sound like much, but done with intention, it is enough to keep the course true.

Chapter 5
Breaking the Worry Spiral

Worry is often mistaken for productive thinking—a kind of mental rehearsal that, if maintained long enough, promises clarity or solutions. In practice, however, prolonged worry rarely solves anything. More often, it functions as an emotional hamster wheel: the scenery of thoughts shifts just enough to feel like progress, yet the underlying uncertainty stubbornly remains in place. The result is an odd mixture of exhaustion and unresolved tension. Ironically, the more pressing the issue seems, the more compulsive the mental looping becomes, as if sheer intensity of attention might compensate for a lack of forward movement. It is precisely this phenomenon—the worry spiral—that this chapter examines in fine detail.

Many attempts to break such a spiral begin with the bluntest of tools: the internal command to "stop worrying." It feels logical, even sensible, but it is fundamentally flawed. Telling the mind to cease thinking about something only makes the thought more persistent—a quirk of cognition well-documented in psychological research. The oft-cited "white bear" experiment illustrates this vividly: participants told not to think of a white bear found the image recurring far more frequently. Emotional thoughts resist suppression; instead of fading, they are flagged as significant, producing a rebound effect. This explains why sheer willpower, absent a subtler method, rarely disrupts the spiral and frequently entrenches it further.

A more effective strategy begins by interrupting worry's autopilot mode. One method, explored later in the chapter, is what we might call label and locate: explicitly naming the anxious thought ("catastrophising about a work presentation," "health-related uncertainty") and identifying where the tension manifests in the body. Naming creates cognitive distance, while locating anchors attention in the physical present. These twin moves shatter the illusion that worry exists purely in the mind, revealing its bodily component and rendering it more manageable. The practice borrows from mindfulness and cognitive-behavioural therapy, yet it is pared down for immediate use—deployable mid-meeting, on a crowded train, or lying awake in the small hours.

For those whose spirals are driven by the fear of losing control over when and how the mind worries, there is a counterintuitive but effective tool: scheduled worry windows. By reserving a set period—say, fifteen minutes in the early evening—for focused rumination, the mind learns to contain and defer worry rather than allowing it to seep unchecked through the day. This reframes worry from an involuntary reflex into a conscious choice, gradually weakening its grip. More importantly, it challenges the assumption that worry must be acted on immediately to have value. In practice, many concerns postponed until the scheduled window lose urgency or significance before the time arrives.

Even these interventions, however, are insufficient without a rapid-response technique for moments when a spiral threatens to dominate. The loop breaker script addresses this need: a concise, rehearsed internal dialogue designed to interrupt thought mid-loop and redirect attention to either deliberate action or postponement. This is not a generic affirmation or motivational slogan; it is a precise, personalised sequence of prompts crafted for immediate recall under pressure. Its aim is not to erase anxiety on command but to restore agency at the moment when the spiral risks deepening.

The strategies discussed in this chapter do not promise serenity, nor do they pretend that uncertainty does not exist. Their purpose is to alter the mechanics of worry so it no longer consumes disproportionate mental space. Breaking a worry spiral is as much about retraining the relationship to thought as it is about addressing the content of thought itself. By moving from seeing worry as a compulsion to viewing it as a signal—something to be managed deliberately rather than indulged reflexively—you create the conditions for a fundamentally different kind of mental clarity.

In the pages ahead, we will examine why the most intuitive anti-worry strategies fail so reliably, how to replace them with methods that harness the brain's own tendencies, and how to operationalise these techniques in daily life so that worry becomes a tool you can pick up and put down, rather than a force that seizes control. The objective is not to eradicate anxiety but to prevent it from dictating the rhythm and scope of your attention. Applied consistently, these methods transform worry from an endless, exhausting loop into a finite process—one that informs action rather than paralyses it.

Why Thought Stopping Fails

The idea of halting a runaway worry by commanding yourself to *stop thinking about it* is as appealing as it is doomed. It feels decisive, a mental equivalent of slamming the brakes. Yet psychological evidence and lived experience converge on the same verdict: the human mind does not yield to suppression in this way. In fact, trying to expel an intrusive thought often makes it return with greater frequency and intensity, a phenomenon recognised for decades in cognitive science. The brain seems to treat any attempt at mental censorship as proof that the thought in question is significant, dangerous, or urgent, thereby amplifying the very mental presence one is trying to erase.

This paradox was famously demonstrated in the 1980s by social psychologist Daniel Wegner, whose "white bear" experiment asked participants to avoid thinking about a white bear for a short period of time. The result was striking: participants reported thinking about the white bear far more often when instructed to suppress the thought than when given no restriction at all. The act of monitoring for the unwanted thought to ensure its absence also acted as a cue, keeping it at the forefront of awareness. This rebound effect is not a quirk of laboratory tasks; it plays out in daily life when someone tries to push away worries about an upcoming exam, an unresolved conflict, or a troubling symptom. The harder the mind is pressed to *not* think about it, the more insistent the thought becomes.

The underlying mechanism is not mysterious. Thought suppression triggers two simultaneous processes: a conscious effort to direct attention elsewhere, and an unconscious monitoring system scanning for any reappearance of the forbidden thought. This scanning process keeps the mental representation primed, meaning even a small trigger—an image, a phrase, a memory fragment—can bring the thought back into full focus. In the case of anxiety, the returning thought often feels sharper, more emotionally charged, as if confirming that it is indeed important. Far from quieting the mind, thought stopping adds a second layer of vigilance to the original concern.

From a neurological perspective, this makes sense. The brain evolved to prioritise potential threats, and a suppressed thought carries all the hallmarks of a possible threat: salience, emotional charge, and uncertainty. Telling yourself *don't think about the meeting tomorrow* is a perfect way to signal to your brain that the meeting is something worth constant monitoring. The amygdala's role in tagging emotionally significant information ensures that avoidance efforts only reinforce the link between the thought and its associated anxiety. This explains why thought stopping is particularly ineffective for worries that involve perceived danger or loss—precisely the kinds of concerns most likely to dominate anxiety spirals.

Even when thought stopping appears to work briefly, the reprieve is fragile. In practice, the mind has not eliminated the thought but has temporarily shifted attention to other stimuli. Because the original thought has not been addressed or reframed, it remains unresolved, ready to resurface. The return often happens in moments of reduced cognitive control: late at night, during routine tasks, or when the mind is fatigued. This cyclical return can breed frustration, as the individual perceives their inability to control the thought as a personal failure, deepening the sense of helplessness that fuels anxiety in the first place.

Real-world examples illustrate how damaging this cycle can be. Consider a professional who receives a vague but urgent-sounding email from their manager: "We need to talk tomorrow." In an effort to avoid spiralling, they tell themselves repeatedly not to think about it, throwing themselves into other work. Yet each pause in activity—waiting for a file to load, walking to the lift—brings the thought back. The avoidance intensifies the uncertainty, and by the time the meeting arrives, the imagined scenarios have grown so extreme that they far exceed the reality of the conversation. The thought stopping has not only failed but has inflated the emotional cost.

The Stoics, writing two millennia before Wegner's experiments, understood this problem intuitively. Epictetus advised not the suppression of thoughts but the examination of them—asking whether they were within one's control, whether they were based on evidence, and whether they were useful to entertain. This ancient insight aligns with modern cognitive-behavioural techniques that advocate replacement and reframing over suppression. The aim is to meet the thought on more constructive terms, transforming it from an adversary into a neutral or even instructive piece of information.

It is worth noting that thought stopping is not always harmful. For trivial or fleeting distractions—such as an irrelevant song lyric intruding during a technical task—quickly directing attention elsewhere may suffice. But when the thought carries emotional weight or links to deeper fears, suppression becomes counterproductive. In these cases, the thought demands processing, not eviction. Recognising this distinction is critical, particularly for those prone to chronic worry.

A more effective alternative begins with acceptance that the thought is present, followed by an intentional choice of response. Labelling the thought ("here's the worry about missing the flight again") creates a degree of detachment, while redirecting attention to a neutral or grounded activity helps weaken its pull. Over time, this approach reduces the thought's capacity to trigger automatic anxiety. The shift is subtle but powerful: instead of battling the mind, you are retraining it.

The failure of thought stopping is not a sign of personal weakness but a feature of human cognition. Our mental machinery is designed to prioritise and rehearse perceived threats, making brute-force suppression a losing strategy when the stakes feel high. By replacing suppression with acknowledgment and deliberate redirection, it is possible to interrupt the spiral without fuelling it. In doing so, you transform the mind's reflexive resistance into a more strategic and sustainable form of control—one that works with the brain's tendencies rather than against them.

Label and Locate

One of the most underestimated skills in dismantling anxiety spirals is the ability to catch a thought in motion, give it a name, and find its coordinates in the body before it recruits more of your mind into its service. Rumination thrives on ambiguity—when an anxious chain of thinking runs without being explicitly recognised, it acquires a sense of inevitability, as if its content were self-evident truth rather than a mental event. By labelling the thought for what it is, and locating its physical echo, you interrupt this unexamined momentum. The act is deceptively simple, but its effects are profound: you convert an abstract worry into something concrete, bounded, and therefore easier to address.

The cognitive value of labelling lies in the separation it creates between the thinker and the thought. Neuroscientific studies on affect labelling—particularly those conducted by Matthew Lieberman and colleagues—demonstrate that putting feelings into words reduces activation in the amygdala, the brain's fear centre, and increases activity in the prefrontal cortex, which governs rational analysis and regulation. In practical terms, saying to yourself, *This is the thought about losing my job* reframes the experience from "I am in danger" to "My brain is generating a danger scenario." This subtle shift in grammatical structure disarms the automatic emotional surge, much as naming an opponent in debate changes the nature of the exchange from ambush to engagement.

Locating the thought in the body serves a complementary purpose. Anxiety is rarely just mental; it broadcasts itself through muscle tension, altered breathing, stomach tightness, a racing pulse, or a prickling in the skin. These sensations can become so fused with the thought that they feel like part of its evidence, convincing you that because your chest feels constricted, the danger must be real. By deliberately scanning the body and identifying where the anxiety sits—*jaw clenched, shoulders hunched, slight nausea*—you create a map. That map allows you to work on the physical state directly through relaxation techniques, posture adjustments, or breath control, while also reminding you that bodily tension is a response, not a prophecy.

Consider a lawyer preparing to present an argument in court. In the hour before the appearance, she notices her mind running through catastrophic scenarios: the judge interrupting her mid-sentence, opposing counsel exploiting a procedural misstep, the client losing confidence. Without labelling, these scenarios blur into a steady emotional fog of "something will go wrong." By stopping to label—*worry about stumbling in argument, worry about being undermined, worry about client reaction*—she transforms an amorphous dread into distinct categories. Locating the sensations—tightness in the throat, heat in the face, shallow breathing—gives her direct targets for intervention. A few rounds of paced breathing to open the chest, loosening her jaw, and straightening her stance begin to reduce the intensity of the physical signal, which in turn softens the urgency of the thoughts.

There is a disciplined humility in this practice. Instead of trying to expel the thought, you acknowledge it in its current form, resisting the temptation to edit, downplay, or argue with it immediately. This preserves cognitive energy and prevents you from being drawn into the kind of mental "courtroom" where your anxious mind will always summon more evidence for the prosecution. By placing the thought under the neutral category of *anxiety episode* or *catastrophic projection*, you sidestep the trap of treating it as a factual report requiring immediate action.

Critically, this is not the same as indulging the thought. Labelling is not the prelude to unpacking every detail of the worry. In fact, it acts as a signal that the thought has been noticed and catalogued, which often diminishes the brain's drive to keep repeating it. Similarly, locating the sensation is not an invitation to dwell on discomfort but a means to recognise it as transient and malleable. This mindset echoes the Stoic emphasis on observing impressions before consenting to them—Marcus Aurelius' reminder to "see things as they are" applied to the internal weather of the mind and body.

Some may resist this method on the grounds that it seems too mechanical, even reductive. Surely there is more to anxiety than tagging it and scanning for muscle tension? The answer is yes—but those additional layers are best addressed once the immediate spiral has been slowed. Labelling and locating are tactical moves: they give you breathing space in which more strategic work—challenging assumptions, aligning with values, choosing a proportionate response—can be done without the distortion of high physiological arousal. Without that initial interruption, the more reflective tools remain out of reach, drowned by the noise of the worry loop.

Over time, the practice can be refined to near-automaticity. With repetition, you may find yourself naming thoughts and noting bodily sensations in real time, sometimes even mid-conversation, without breaking the flow. This fluency matters, because anxiety often strikes in moments where pausing for a formal exercise is impractical. A manager fielding a hostile question in a meeting can silently register, *this is the thought about looking incompetent*, notice the knot in the stomach, and respond with measured composure rather than defensiveness. The skill becomes a background process, akin to a driver adjusting their grip on the wheel without conscious deliberation.

The interplay between labelling and locating also deepens self-knowledge. Patterns emerge: certain themes recur in your worries, certain muscles bear the brunt of tension, certain settings amplify the link between thought and sensation. This data can guide preventative action—addressing known triggers, strengthening coping strategies, and noticing early warning signs before a spiral gathers speed. In this way, the method moves from reactive to proactive, becoming not just a tool for disrupting rumination but a compass for maintaining mental equilibrium.

What makes this approach powerful is not complexity but precision. Anxiety often wins because it operates on vague terms and broad generalities; labelling and locating collapse that vagueness into specifics. A specific thought is less overwhelming than an amorphous cloud of dread. A specific muscle tension is easier to release than a general sense of "I'm on edge." By rendering the intangible tangible, you take the first, critical step in reclaiming control from a process that thrives in the shadows of unexamined awareness.

Worry Windows

The idea that you can *schedule* your anxiety may sound counterintuitive, even absurd. Worry feels involuntary—something that descends without warning and refuses to be reasoned with. Yet the human mind, while prone to compulsive rumination, is also remarkably responsive to structure. One of the most effective ways to weaken a worry spiral is not to demand its immediate cessation, but to defer it to a dedicated time and place: a *worry window*. This is a bounded period in which you allow yourself to think through concerns deliberately, on your terms, and outside the heat of impulsive reaction. By containing worry in this way, you reassert control over its timing and scope, shifting from a position of being hounded by thoughts to managing them as scheduled tasks.

The psychological rationale behind worry windows is rooted in the principles of stimulus control and attentional training. In cognitive behavioural therapy (CBT), particularly in its application for generalised anxiety disorder, clinicians often assign patients a fixed "worry period" of fifteen to thirty minutes once or twice daily. During this time, the patient is instructed to actively consider whatever is troubling them—no censorship, no premature resolution required—but to postpone all other worry episodes until that window arrives. This act of postponement disrupts the automatic link between an intrusive thought and an immediate spiral, teaching the brain that anxiety does not demand instant engagement. Over weeks of consistent practice, the frequency and intensity of intrusive thoughts often diminish, precisely because the brain no longer treats them as urgent.

A practical example illustrates the shift. Imagine a project manager overseeing a high-stakes client account. In the middle of reviewing emails, she is struck by a sudden fear: *What if the client pulls out?* Her habitual response might be to abandon her work to mentally simulate every possible scenario—contracts collapsing, reputational damage, the logistics of staff reallocation. Instead, she notes the thought, writes it down, and tells herself, *I will review this at 5:30 p.m. during my worry window.* The thought does not vanish immediately—it may recur—but each time it does, she redirects it to the same appointment. When the scheduled time arrives, she deliberately engages with it: assessing probability, considering contingencies, and deciding whether action is required. Over time, the reflex to chase the thought immediately weakens, replaced by the habit of postponement.

The power of worry windows lies in two related mechanisms. First, they weaken the urgency bias of anxious thinking. Worries often feel compelling not because they are inherently important, but because the mind has learned to treat them as signals that demand immediate processing. Postponement teaches that not every signal is an alarm. Second, they create a psychological container. Just as a meeting has a start and end time, a worry window defines the limits of engagement, preventing concerns from expanding to fill the day. Even chronic worriers report that by the time the window arrives, some of the thoughts they meant to review have already lost their charge or have resolved themselves.

There is also a paradoxical advantage to scheduled worrying: it can make thinking about problems more productive. When worries arrive at random, they tend to be fragmentary and repetitive, circling the same "what if" without resolution. In a structured window, the mind approaches them with more composure and a fuller cognitive toolkit. You can examine evidence, weigh probabilities, and generate practical options rather than looping through the same fearful imagery. *Containment turns worry from a reflex into a conscious exercise.*

Critics sometimes object that deferring worry risks neglecting urgent issues. This concern is valid in cases where a thought signals immediate action—smelling smoke, seeing an unsafe driver on the road, receiving a critical systems alert. Worry windows are not a substitute for responding to genuine emergencies. They are designed for recurring, speculative concerns that rarely require instant resolution—financial "what ifs," health anxieties without current symptoms, interpersonal insecurities. In fact, by training the brain to distinguish between true emergencies and hypothetical ones, the practice sharpens situational judgment.

Adopting worry windows does demand initial discipline, and resistance is common. The anxious mind insists that if you do not think about the issue now, you will lose your chance to prepare. This is the same reasoning that fuels compulsions in obsessive-compulsive disorder—the fear of delayed engagement creating more anxiety than the problem itself. The skill is in tolerating that initial discomfort, knowing that the act of postponement is itself part of the treatment. The more consistently you honour the boundary, the more your mind accepts that it is safe to defer.

Interestingly, the concept is not purely modern. Stoic philosophy advised time-bounding emotional engagement: Marcus Aurelius counselled himself to limit his attention to the present task, resisting the pull of speculative distress. The difference is that modern worry windows embrace, rather than suppress, the act of consideration—but they do so under controlled conditions. This approach avoids the rebound effect of thought suppression, where trying not to think about something paradoxically makes it more persistent.

Over weeks or months, you may notice two distinct changes. First, the total volume of worry decreases, because not every intrusive thought feels worth bringing to the scheduled session. Second, the quality of the remaining worry improves: it becomes more solution-focused and less repetitive. For some, this is accompanied by a greater sense of mental space, the ability to enjoy periods of genuine presence without the constant tug of unresolved concerns. This is not because life has become simpler, but because the mental process for handling its uncertainties has become more deliberate.

Ultimately, worry windows shift the balance of power. Anxiety thrives in a system where it sets the timetable; scheduled periods reverse this dynamic. You cannot stop your mind from generating scenarios, but you can decide when and how to engage with them. This reframing—*I am not avoiding the thought; I am choosing its time*—is a subtle but potent reassertion of agency. It reinforces the principle that mental clarity is not the absence of troubling thoughts, but the capacity to place them in their rightful context.

Loop Breaker Script

There is a distinct moment in any worry spiral when you are no longer evaluating reality—you are feeding an echo chamber of your own making. The conversation in your head is no longer about the facts at hand, but about the feared implications of those facts, and then the feared implications of *those* implications, until the original concern is almost unrecognisable. Left unchecked, the mind can run this loop indefinitely, burning cognitive energy while producing no new insight. What interrupts this process is not forceful suppression—telling yourself to "just stop" rarely works—but the deliberate insertion of a short, clear, and repeatable internal script that severs the momentum of the spiral without demanding instant emotional calm. The point is not to win an argument with your anxiety, but to reclaim the steering wheel from it.

A well-crafted loop breaker script works on several levels at once. It acts as a cognitive cue to recognise that you are *in* the spiral; it provides an alternative track for attention to follow; and it disrupts the reward cycle that fuels repetitive thinking. The most effective scripts are neither elaborate affirmations nor aggressive commands. They are concise, declarative statements that orient you to the present, affirm agency, and establish the irrelevance of further rumination in this moment. Their brevity matters: in the heat of a mental loop, working memory is already taxed, and a lengthy, complex mantra risks becoming one more thought to spiral around.

Consider a client I worked with, a litigation lawyer accustomed to high-pressure deadlines. When a case took a surprising turn, she found herself repeatedly replaying a single conversation with opposing counsel, each time imagining how she *should* have responded. These mental reruns absorbed hours, disrupted her focus, and eroded her sleep. We developed a script: *This is a replay, not reality. I choose to brief my mind later.* The first clause labelled the experience accurately—she was watching a mental tape, not engaging with the present case. The second clause established a choice and a boundary, postponing analysis to a specific time. Over weeks, the act of deploying this script shortened her spirals from hours to minutes, not because the anxiety was eliminated, but because it no longer had free rein to loop unchecked.

For many, the resistance to using a loop breaker script lies in the belief that the worry is productive—*If I stop now, I'll miss something important.* But loops are deceptive in this way: they feel active, even purposeful, yet they tend to recycle the same narrow range of thoughts without uncovering anything new. The script functions as a truth test—if there is truly something actionable, it can be addressed later in a structured review, such as a scheduled problem-solving session or a "worry window." If there isn't, the spiral is nothing more than mental noise, and disengagement is a gain, not a loss.

A loop breaker script is not a one-size-fits-all tool; its effectiveness depends on tone, personal relevance, and the specific triggers that tend to trap the mind. Some people respond well to a factual, almost clinical phrasing: *This is a thought, not an emergency.* Others prefer a slightly directive tone: *Not useful right now—park it.* The best scripts are crafted in the language you naturally use, not in the language you think "should" work. Authenticity is essential, because the brain recognises when a phrase is rote and disregards it.

The practice gains strength when paired with an immediate, simple action. After delivering the script internally, shifting your sensory focus—standing up, feeling your feet on the floor, or engaging your hands in a physical task—provides the body-level reset that consolidates the interruption. This is not about distraction for its own sake, but about anchoring the mind in stimuli that compete effectively with the spiral's momentum. In neuroscience terms, you are recruiting bottom-up sensory processing to override the top-down cognitive loop.

Sceptics sometimes argue that a brief phrase cannot possibly dismantle deeply entrenched anxiety patterns. It is true that no single tool works universally, and that for some individuals, spirals are tied to complex trauma or severe anxiety disorders requiring multi-pronged interventions. But dismissing the loop breaker as too simple misunderstands its role: it is not a cure in itself, but a precision tool for interrupting acute mental inertia, making space for more deliberate problem-solving or calming techniques. Its simplicity is precisely what allows it to be remembered and deployed under stress.

Historical and cross-cultural practices reinforce this principle. Mindfulness traditions use short "noting" labels—*thinking, worrying, remembering*—to puncture the trance of identification with thought.

Certain military mental conditioning programmes use clipped verbal cues to break fixation under pressure, such as *reset* or *switch*. In both cases, the brevity of the phrase is key to cutting through cognitive clutter. The loop breaker script is simply a tailored, personal version of this mechanism, designed for the civilian contexts of work, relationships, and everyday decision-making.

The deeper benefit of using such a script is cumulative. At first, it may feel awkward or even futile to repeat a set phrase in your head while emotions are high. But with repetition, you develop what could be called *metacognitive reflexes*—the capacity to recognise thought patterns and intervene automatically before they escalate. This is the psychological equivalent of a driver hitting the brakes at the first sign of a skid, rather than waiting until the car has veered dangerously off course. Over time, this self-interruption doesn't just end spirals faster; it prevents many from starting at all.

Ultimately, the loop breaker script is a small intervention with outsized leverage. It is not about silencing the mind forever or pretending that anxiety has no place. It is about refusing to let thought spirals monopolise your finite cognitive and emotional bandwidth. By condensing your interruption into a single, practiced line, you make it portable, repeatable, and resistant to the very momentum it is designed to stop. And in that moment—whether you are at your desk, lying awake at night, or standing in a crowded train—you take back the one thing a spiral always tries to steal: the ability to choose what happens next.

Chapter 6
The Stoic Reframe

Stress rarely exists in isolation; it is shaped as much by the lens through which we view events as by the events themselves. A missed deadline, a fraught conversation, an unexpected bill—none of these are inherently catastrophic, yet they can feel overwhelming when magnified by our own interpretation. The Stoics grasped that perspective is not a philosophical indulgence but a practical instrument for composure. They trained themselves to shift viewpoints, question initial reactions, and resist the tyranny of immediacy. This chapter explores how similar reframing techniques can be applied today—not to deny difficulty, but to strip away the unnecessary suffering that often accompanies it.

Consider the View from Above, a Stoic exercise in mental elevation. One imagines stepping back from the immediate scene: first observing it from the ceiling, then the street, the city, and ultimately from the vantage of the Earth itself. From such heights, daily crises shrink to their true proportion. The irate email becomes a tiny data point in the vast network of human communication; the awkward meeting, a momentary blip across decades. This is not detachment as apathy, but detachment as scale: the capacity to see the broader picture. Neuroscience might describe it as activating higher-order cognitive control to modulate the amygdala's rapid threat signalling—ancient philosophy converging with modern brain science.

Where the View from Above shifts the visual frame, reframing from "threat" to "challenge" shifts the verbal one. Language—even our internal dialogue—guides physiological response. Label a situation as a "threat," and the body braces defensively: tightened muscles, narrowed attention, a bias toward avoidance. Call it a "challenge," and the body still mobilises energy, but the mind leans toward engagement and problem-solving. Athletes, surgeons, and negotiators frequently deploy this reframing, often without conscious thought, turning pressure into performance. For those prone to anxiety, practising this linguistic shift transforms stress from something merely to endure into something to tackle with skill.

Another Stoic-inspired approach is the Temporary Truth Test, which interrogates anxious predictions. Worry often assumes permanence: this problem will define my life. Reality, however, rarely cooperates with such absolutes. Asking "Will this matter in a month? A year? Five years?" dismantles the illusion of foreverness that fuels emotional overload. This is not a dismissal of genuine hardship but a tool to distinguish fleeting difficulties from identity-defining catastrophes. Frequently, what feels permanent is transient, and recognising that passage helps prevent catastrophising from taking root.

Historical Humility offers yet another lens. It calls attention to the resilience of humans across eras far harsher than our own: the siege of Athens, the plagues of Rome, philosophers exiled under oppressive regimes. These episodes are not mere curiosities; they are the crucibles in which Stoic thought was forged. The intention is not to trivialise contemporary struggles but to remind ourselves that resilience is a deeply human inheritance. If people under far harsher conditions could preserve dignity, agency, and moral clarity, then the same capacities exist within us, ready to be activated.

What unites these methods is their challenge to the automatic interpretations our minds generate under stress. Left unexamined, these interpretations narrow options, inflate threats, and prolong distress. Viewed through a Stoic lens, however, they become malleable—subject to choice rather than reflex. The Stoic Reframe does not promise instantaneous serenity, but it offers a disciplined way of seeing, making composure far more attainable. In the following chapters, we will practise these shifts—visual, verbal, temporal, and historical—until reframing becomes less an emergency manoeuvre and more a habitual lens. The goal is not to live in denial of hardship but to confront it with the clarity and steadiness of someone who chooses wisely, sees fully, and refuses to be ruled by the first story the mind tells.

View from Above – A cognitive shift technique to deflate immediate stress by seeing the larger context

A mind caught in the heat of stress narrows its field of vision. Threats loom larger than they are, small obstacles inflate to insurmountable barriers, and the present moment feels like the entire map of existence. The Stoic exercise known as the *View from Above* dismantles this distortion not by urging us to "calm down" or "think positive," but by altering the scale at which we perceive our lives. It is a deliberate act of mental altitude gain: moving from the confined room of our current perspective to a higher vantage point where context, proportion, and perspective reassert themselves. This is not an abstract thought experiment; it is a technique that can be practised in minutes and whose utility is as relevant to a harried executive in 2025 as it was to a philosopher under siege in ancient Rome.

At its core, the View from Above asks you to imagine rising above your immediate circumstances. Start by picturing yourself in the room where you sit, then mentally pull back until you see the building, the street, the city, the surrounding countryside. Keep pulling back—past national borders, over oceans, into the curvature of the Earth itself. Soon, the entire planet rests in view, and your present concern is no longer a suffocating reality but a pinpoint within a vast, interdependent system. When viewed from that scale, most of the intensity we assign to events is revealed as a function of our vantage point, not the events themselves. Cognitive science offers an explanation: perspective-taking engages brain regions involved in metacognition and self-regulation, quieting the amygdala-driven urgency that fuels stress. The Stoics discovered this without fMRI scans, but with equal clarity—they knew that *emotional proportion is a matter of perceptual proportion.*

This shift in scale is not about dismissing problems but right-sizing them. An impending performance review can feel like a personal referendum when viewed from within the confines of one's own anxiety. Yet from the orbital vantage point of the exercise, it becomes one of many conversations happening on one of billions of inhabited days, across a planet whose history dwarfs any single exchange. The effect is humbling without being demeaning: you are not *nothing*, but you are not the entire picture either. This balance tempers both ego-driven panic and self-defeating despair. As Marcus Aurelius wrote in his *Meditations*, "You could leave life right now. Let that determine what you do and say and think." The View from Above sharpens that awareness—not to induce fatalism, but to strip away the false urgency that obscures what actually matters.

Real-world application of this mental technique is surprisingly practical. Consider an emergency room doctor facing a cascade of critical cases. In the heat of triage, it is easy to slip into tunnel vision, where every beep, every shout, every decision feels monumental. Yet seasoned clinicians often describe a paradoxical calm that comes from mentally "zooming out," seeing the flow of the shift rather than each isolated moment. The skill lies in toggling between micro-focus (necessary for immediate action) and macro-perspective (necessary for sustained performance). The View from Above is a conscious rehearsal of that toggle. By practising it outside crisis moments, you train your nervous system to recover proportion more quickly when stakes feel high.

The technique also helps disentangle personal identity from situational stress. If you fail at a project, lose an argument, or make an error, zooming out reminds you that the self is not synonymous with the event. You are a participant in a much larger network of causes and effects, many beyond your control. This is not an excuse for irresponsibility but a grounding reminder that one setback does not define the arc of your life. Leaders who can sustain this broader perspective are less likely to overreact to fluctuations in fortune, and more likely to make measured decisions that align with long-term priorities rather than short-term relief.

Critics might object that such mental distancing risks detachment from meaningful engagement—that by repeatedly reframing problems as small in the grand scheme, we risk underestimating their significance in the present. This is where the nuance of the Stoic approach matters. The View from Above is not about minimising suffering or moral responsibility; it is about removing distortion so we can act more effectively. By seeing your current problem as *one part* of a much larger system, you can respond without panic and allocate your energy with greater precision. It is the difference between acknowledging a storm and assuming the entire climate has changed forever.

The exercise also serves as an antidote to the chronic myopia encouraged by modern media. News cycles, social feeds, and hyperlocal crises compete for our attention, each presented as if it is the decisive turning point of civilisation. From the altitude of the

View from Above, we recognise patterns: that public outrage has always existed, that geopolitical tensions rise and fall, that personal hardships are mirrored in countless other lives. This recognition does not numb us to suffering; it makes us less susceptible to manipulation by immediacy. When you understand that every "breaking news" headline is one thread in a centuries-long fabric, you are less likely to let it dictate your emotional weather for the day.

There is also a contemplative dimension to the exercise that deepens resilience over time. By repeatedly imagining yourself as a tiny part of the whole, you cultivate a humility that protects against both arrogance in victory and despair in defeat. The Stoics were not the only ones to practise this—Buddhist teachings on impermanence, astronaut accounts of the "overview effect," and even certain military leadership programmes echo the same core insight: *the way you see the world changes what you are capable of within it.* Astronauts who have viewed Earth from space often describe a profound shift in priorities, feeling a greater sense of unity and a reduced tolerance for petty conflicts. The Stoic exercise aims to evoke a similar shift without the need for a rocket launch.

Ultimately, the View from Above is about reclaiming authorship over your emotional scale. Stress thrives when the frame is too tight, when the edges of a problem press up against the edges of your identity. By consciously expanding that frame, you give yourself room to think, to breathe, and to choose. This is not an escape from reality but a recalibration of it—one that allows for both immediate action and enduring calm. The next time you feel trapped inside the walls of your own stress, remember that the walls are not fixed. They are drawn by perspective, and perspective is a choice.

Shifting from Threat to Challenge – Uses language reframing to alter stress perception

The human nervous system is exquisitely tuned to detect threat, but far less adept at distinguishing between what is dangerous and what is simply demanding. A difficult conversation with a manager, an upcoming presentation, or a competitive interview can all trigger the same physiological stress responses that evolved for escaping predators. The problem is not just biological—it is also linguistic.

How we *name* an experience often dictates how we respond to it. Calling a situation a "threat" primes the body and mind for avoidance, hypervigilance, and defensive behaviour. Calling it a "challenge" primes us for engagement, problem-solving, and growth. The reframing is not cosmetic; it alters the underlying stress response itself.

Psychologists have found that the labels we attach to stress are not neutral descriptors but active shapers of perception. In studies on stress appraisal, participants who were instructed to interpret their racing heart and quickened breath before a task as signs of readiness—not danger—showed improved performance, lower anxiety, and more resilient cardiovascular responses. This aligns with what Stoic thinkers recognised centuries ago: *events are not inherently good or bad; our interpretations give them their weight.* In modern terms, language can be a lever for emotional regulation. The shift from "I'm under attack" to "I'm under test" is subtle yet transformative.

This is not about forced optimism or sugar-coating hardship. Some situations are genuinely hazardous, and labelling them otherwise would be delusional. The value of the threat-to-challenge shift lies in contexts where our physiological arousal is disproportionate to the actual risk. Public speaking is the classic example: for most people, it poses no real danger to life or livelihood, yet it is ranked among the top fears in surveys worldwide. By consciously reframing the event as an opportunity to communicate ideas, persuade an audience, or sharpen a skill, we change the lens through which the brain predicts outcomes—and in doing so, we soften the grip of performance anxiety.

The language shift also changes the scope of agency we perceive. Threat language narrows our behavioural repertoire. When we tell ourselves "I can't handle this" or "This will go badly," the brain's problem-solving capacities constrict, focusing instead on escape or minimisation. Challenge language widens that repertoire by presupposing capacity and inviting action. Saying "This will test my skills" or "This is a chance to improve" implies the possibility of a constructive outcome. The subtle implication that we can meet the demand activates curiosity alongside caution—a much more productive blend for high-pressure situations.

Consider the way elite athletes speak before a competition. Rarely do they describe an opponent as a looming danger; more often they frame the contest as a proving ground or a chance to demonstrate training. This reframing does not erase the stakes, but it channels arousal into focus rather than paralysis. The same approach can be applied in high-stakes professions outside sport. Surgeons, firefighters, negotiators, and military officers are trained to reframe intense scenarios as challenges to be met with skill, rather than threats to be survived. The language they use under pressure is a deliberate tool, not a passive habit.

It is worth noting that language reframing operates best when it is embedded in consistent practice. Changing a single word in the heat of panic is unlikely to override years of habitual threat appraisal. However, incorporating challenge framing into daily self-talk builds a default mode that is easier to access when stress spikes. This might involve pre-emptively naming a daunting project as "a worthwhile stretch" rather than "an ordeal" or reinterpreting criticism as "data for refinement" rather than "evidence of failure." Over time, such linguistic habits recondition the association between stress cues and behavioural readiness.

Critics sometimes argue that reframing risks trivialising real difficulties, particularly in contexts of systemic or chronic stress. There is truth to this caution—no amount of verbal finesse can erase genuine danger or injustice. Yet even in sustained adversity, the framing of stress can influence resilience. For example, medical professionals working in resource-strapped environments often report that framing their workload as a challenge to their ingenuity, rather than a threat to their competence, sustains them through extended crises. The reframing does not deny hardship; it reshapes the inner posture with which they face it.

From a neurological perspective, this makes sense. When stress is perceived as a challenge, the hypothalamic–pituitary–adrenal (HPA) axis is activated in a way that supports sustained performance without tipping into the immune suppression and cognitive impairment associated with threat states. Heart rate and cortisol may still rise, but they do so in a pattern that is less damaging and more adaptive. In short, the body behaves differently when the mind believes the situation is conquerable. Language is the bridge between perception and physiology.

The Stoics would have recognised this as an exercise in deliberate judgment. Epictetus reminded his students that "People are disturbed not by things, but by the views which they take of them." To the Stoic, the aim was not to deny the difficulty of life but to adopt interpretations that fostered agency and virtue. Reframing threat as challenge is precisely this—acknowledging the obstacle while refusing to grant it the power to dictate one's stance.

Applied consistently, the shift from threat to challenge has a compounding effect. At first, it may feel like a conscious, even awkward intervention: catching yourself mid-thought and replacing "I'm in trouble" with "I'm being tested." With repetition, it becomes a reflex, reshaping both self-talk and behaviour. The benefit is not merely emotional comfort but expanded capacity. A challenge mindset encourages preparation, learning, and adaptation—qualities that are essential not only for surviving stress but for thriving in its presence.

Ultimately, the reframing of stress from threat to challenge is not a linguistic trick; it is a recalibration of identity. It says, implicitly, "I am the kind of person who faces into difficulty." That is a stance which strengthens over time, and one which fundamentally changes the relationship between stress and performance. By controlling the words we use to describe our circumstances, we begin to control the way those circumstances control us.

The Temporary Truth Test – Helps question the permanence of anxious predictions

One of anxiety's most convincing tricks is its insistence that the future it imagines is fixed and inevitable. The mind, once caught in this loop, stops treating its predictions as possibilities and begins holding them as certainties. "I will fail this exam," "This deal will collapse," "They will think less of me"—phrases that start as worries harden into mental headlines. What is often missed is that these headlines are time-stamped with the present moment's emotions.

Anxiety makes a temporary perception feel like a permanent fact. The Temporary Truth Test is a way of pulling those predictions back into the light, where they can be questioned, reframed, and sometimes dismantled altogether.

This technique hinges on a deceptively simple insight: *most predictions are not truths—they are working hypotheses built under emotional strain.* Yet in the grip of anxiety, the distinction between hypothesis and certainty blurs. Asking whether what you believe will still be true in a week, a month, or a year forces a shift from emotional immediacy to a broader temporal perspective. This is not about suppressing feelings; it is about reintroducing proportion. Just as historians assess events with the benefit of hindsight, the anxious thinker can project forward and ask whether the feared outcome will matter in the long arc of their life.

The effectiveness of this test is not speculative—it aligns with decades of research in cognitive behavioural therapy showing that catastrophic thinking often collapses when subjected to temporal distancing. In one study, individuals prone to anxiety were asked to reframe immediate worries as questions about the long-term. Those who did reported reduced intensity of distress and increased problem-solving ability. This is because time reframing interrupts the brain's threat circuitry by undermining the sense of urgency that fuels anxious loops. When a fear is imagined at a future distance, it is stripped of some of its immediacy, and the mind can examine it without the same chemical load of cortisol and adrenaline.

Real-world application is straightforward but requires practice. Imagine an employee convinced that a critical email from their manager signals impending dismissal. In the moment, this feels not just plausible but inevitable. Applying the Temporary Truth Test might involve asking: "Will this email still matter in six months?" That question, far from minimising the issue, invites a more rational examination. Perhaps the employee recalls previous instances when terse emails led to constructive discussions rather than punitive action. The test does not guarantee reassurance, but it creates enough cognitive space to prevent reflexive panic from dictating behaviour.

The Stoics, too, understood this principle, though expressed in different terms. Marcus Aurelius frequently reminded himself to view life's troubles as passing, noting that "all is ephemeral—both the rememberer and the remembered." This perspective was not nihilistic; it was a deliberate antidote to the mind's tendency to inflate the present's importance. By recognising that today's crises are tomorrow's anecdotes—or forgotten entirely—one can resist the urge to act as if the current emotional weather is permanent climate.

The Temporary Truth Test also guards against the opposite distortion: the belief that current relief will last forever. This matters because some anxious predictions are not about danger but about the fear of losing something good—a relationship, health, status. By acknowledging that pleasant states are also temporary, we reduce the shock when they inevitably change. This balanced application prevents the test from becoming a mere comfort tool and grounds it instead in realistic appraisal of life's transience.

One challenge in applying this technique is that anxiety often resists it with a counter-argument: "Even if it won't matter in a year, it matters now." That is partially true—many things do matter in the short term. But here the test works not by denying current relevance but by scaling the threat to its appropriate time frame. A client facing a project deadline might still need to work hard today, but recognising that the stress will fade can prevent overinvestment of emotional energy that drains resilience for future challenges.

Interestingly, the test has a physiological counterpart in how the brain processes narrative time. When we imagine ourselves in the future, different neural networks activate than when we focus on immediate threat. The shift engages the medial prefrontal cortex and posterior cingulate cortex—regions associated with perspective-taking and autobiographical memory—rather than exclusively triggering the amygdala's alarm system. In other words, by asking whether a fear is a temporary truth, we are engaging brain systems built for reflection instead of reaction.

Practical refinement can make the Temporary Truth Test more potent. Some find it helpful to pair the question with a physical gesture, such as stepping back from a desk, looking out of a window, or even standing up to change posture. This creates a behavioural cue that reinforces the mental shift. Others keep a written record of past "permanent" predictions that turned out to be temporary, reviewing them as a way of building evidence against the mind's tendency to forecast doom with absolute confidence. Over time, such a log becomes an archive of disproven anxieties—a tangible argument against the permanence illusion.

Critics might argue that the test risks complacency. If one believes that all problems are temporary, might that not undermine urgency and responsibility? The answer lies in balance. The Temporary Truth Test is not a licence for inaction but a tool for proportion. It allows us to engage with challenges without granting them the status of unalterable fate. The aim is not detachment but right-sizing—giving events the weight they deserve, neither more nor less.

Perhaps the most powerful aspect of this technique is that it reintroduces choice. Anxiety thrives in conditions where the mind feels trapped, as if the predicted outcome is both fixed and unavoidable. By reframing the fear as a temporary truth—subject to change, context, and influence—we remind ourselves that we can act in ways that shape the future rather than merely brace for it. This act of mental repositioning does not eliminate uncertainty, but it converts it from an enemy into a field of possibility.

When applied consistently, the Temporary Truth Test becomes less of an isolated exercise and more of a habit of mind. It creates a default stance of curiosity toward one's own fears: *Is this truly permanent, or just how it feels today?* That question alone can puncture the closed loop of anxious certainty, replacing it with something quieter but more enduring—a willingness to wait, to watch, and to see what actually happens.

Historical Humility – Draws parallels to Stoic resilience during crises far worse than modern fears

Perspective is a luxury rarely afforded in the middle of anxiety, yet it is one of the most potent antidotes to its distortions. Historical humility—deliberately placing our personal fears against the backdrop of human endurance across centuries—can puncture the inflated sense of uniqueness and severity that often accompanies our present troubles. This is not an exercise in dismissing hardship, but in recalibrating its scale. When Marcus Aurelius wrote *"You could leave life right now. Let that determine what you do and say and think,"* he was not speaking from a life of abstract philosophy. He was leading an empire beset by invasions, famine, and a plague that killed millions. And yet, he counselled composure, discipline, and a refusal to surrender agency to fear.

Modern anxieties—whether about economic instability, health concerns, or professional setbacks—are real in their personal impact, but they rarely match the existential weight of the crises endured by those before us. Consider the Antonine Plague, which raged for over a decade in the late 2nd century AD. Historical accounts suggest mortality rates so high that whole towns were depopulated. Public life, commerce, and military campaigns were crippled. For the Stoics of that era, resilience was not optional—it was a daily discipline of confronting uncertainty without yielding to paralysis. They had no vaccines, no robust medical system, and no global relief infrastructure. Yet they left us writings that breathe with clarity, moral focus, and a refusal to be defined by dread.

The relevance to our own age is direct. Anxiety convinces us that *this* moment—this difficulty, this uncertainty—is somehow unprecedented in its threat. Historical humility undermines that illusion by reminding us that humanity has faced, survived, and often grown through catastrophes far greater in scale. This is not to belittle modern challenges, but to contextualise them. To a Roman citizen who had just buried half their family, the inconvenience of a delayed project or a critical comment from a colleague would barely register. This is the lens that the Stoics invite us to adopt: not one of dismissiveness, but of proportion.

Proportion changes the emotional chemistry of fear. When we place our current problem beside the Siege of Jerusalem in 70 CE, or the winter at Valley Forge, or the London Blitz, the mind cannot sustain the same intensity of panic without feeling the absurdity of its own scale distortion. The soldiers at Valley Forge endured sub-zero temperatures, disease, and starvation, yet Washington's correspondence from that time is laced with encouragement, resolve, and strategy—not the language of collapse. Similarly, Londoners during the Blitz navigated daily bombings by holding onto routines, humour, and social solidarity. There was fear, but it did not become the organising principle of their lives.

Stoic resilience in these historical contexts was not about blind optimism. It was about an unflinching acceptance of reality, paired with a commitment to live well within it. Epictetus, born into slavery and later crippled, taught his students that "It's not things themselves that disturb us, but our judgments about them." Applied to historical humility, this means that the difference between despair and steadiness lies not in the absence of threat but in the framing of it. If our ancestors could hold their dignity while facing famine, siege, and plague, perhaps we can hold ours in the face of a volatile market or a delayed diagnosis.

Critics might argue that invoking the severity of past crises risks dismissing the emotional validity of current struggles. That risk is real if historical humility is applied crudely—as a blunt "others had it worse" dismissal. The Stoic application, however, is subtler. It does not seek to invalidate feeling, but to broaden the frame in which that feeling is held. If your fear is a storm, history is the coastline on which countless storms have broken and receded. This wider view does not end discomfort, but it can stop fear from masquerading as fate.

There is also a cognitive advantage here. Anxiety thrives in the narrow present, where the mind loops endlessly over perceived threats. Historical perspective forces a temporal expansion. It draws the mind into a timeline in which this moment is one of many—not the sum total of reality. That shift alone can weaken the claustrophobic grip of panic. It is harder to see a single event as world-ending when history reminds you that the world has ended many times for others and yet, here you stand.

Practical application of historical humility can be as simple as building a mental library of historical episodes and lives that exemplify resilience. When facing a stressful situation, one might recall Admiral James Stockdale, imprisoned and tortured for over seven years during the Vietnam War, who drew directly on Stoic philosophy to survive. Or Nelson Mandela, who endured 27 years of imprisonment without allowing bitterness to dominate his purpose. These are not meant to be heroic distractions from one's own challenges, but models of the human capacity to endure without surrendering to despair.

The Stoics themselves used this kind of comparative thinking not as a comfort blanket but as a discipline. Seneca often wrote to Lucilius about men who had faced far greater trials with fortitude, urging him to use their example as proof that fear can be mastered. The exercise was not meant to make one feel small, but to make one feel part of an unbroken human tradition of confronting uncertainty with courage. In this sense, historical humility is less about diminishing your suffering and more about enlarging your sense of connection to those who have walked harder roads.

When applied regularly, this practice reshapes the narrative of anxiety. Instead of "This is unbearable," the inner voice shifts towards "Others have borne worse, and I can bear this." That is not denial—it is solidarity across time. It reframes endurance as an inherited skill, something we are capable of because we belong to a lineage that has already proven it possible. This is perhaps the most radical insight of historical humility: it changes the question from "Why me?" to "Why not me?" In doing so, it transforms adversity from a personal insult into a shared human condition, and resilience from a rare virtue into a natural expectation.

Chapter 7
Handling the Body's Alarm

Anxiety is not confined to the mind; it broadcasts itself through the body, manifesting in racing heartbeats, shallow breaths, taut muscles, and an uneasy gut. For many, the challenge is less the thoughts that accompany fear than the raw, visceral impression it leaves on the body. These physical sensations can be remarkably persuasive—a rapid pulse feels like immediate danger, tightness in the chest feels like a warning, and shallow breathing feels suffocating. Yet much of this alarm is miscalibrated, a survival mechanism misfiring in boardrooms, family dinners, or in the quiet of night. The task, then, is not to suppress these signals but to recalibrate how we interpret and respond to them.

The body's alarm system evolved for decisive action: a flicker in the grass might signal a predator, a sudden noise in the dark a real threat. The physiological cascade—the familiar fight-or-flight reaction—remains unchanged, even though our environment has shifted beyond recognition. Modern threats are rarely literal predators; they come as a terse email, a looming deadline, or the possibility of a troubling medical result. These situations demand reasoning, not sprinting, yet the body often fails to distinguish between the two. Once the amygdala—the brain's emotional sentinel—perceives danger, the cascade begins. For some, this response is hair-trigger: the body reacts as though the world is aflame when it is, in fact, a minor inconvenience.

Central to this process is prediction error. The brain is constantly forecasting what will happen next, and when those forecasts skew catastrophic, the body responds accordingly. Anxiety feels persuasive because the physical sensations seem like evidence of threat, when they are often evidence of miscalculation. If the body is a fire alarm, anxiety is the smoke detector that goes off every time toast burns. Learning to detect and correct these errors—without smashing the alarm—is essential. Merely telling oneself "calm down" rarely works; it ignores the physiological arousal driving the perception of danger.

Intentional physical interventions—reset routines—become crucial here. These are not abstract mindfulness platitudes but concrete adjustments in breathing, posture, and movement that alter chemical signalling in the body. By interrupting runaway sympathetic activation, you reduce the fuel that panic feeds upon. This is not about fooling the mind into believing all is well, but about giving the mind less physiological panic to interpret. Because brain and body operate in a continuous feedback loop, changing one invariably shifts the other.

For some, the bodily sensations themselves trigger anxiety. A pounding heart, sweaty palms, or a tight jaw can be dreaded in advance, leading to avoidance that heightens sensitivity over time. Interoceptive exposure addresses this: instead of fleeing from uncomfortable sensations, you learn to encounter them in controlled, safe contexts until their threat diminishes. It is the physiological equivalent of wading into a shallow wave repeatedly until you realise it cannot sweep you away. The process is deliberate, gradual, and sometimes uncomfortable, but it remains one of the most effective ways to separate bodily arousal from catastrophic interpretation.

Even with careful practice, the body cannot sustain heightened alert indefinitely without consequence. Chronic activation sensitises the nervous system, making it more prone to false alarms. This is why physical recovery windows are vital—deliberate, protected periods where heart rate, breathing, and muscle tone can settle. These are not indulgences but essential intervals, creating conditions for the alarm system to recalibrate. Recovery is not passive; it is an active environment in which the body relearns safety.

This chapter provides a framework for reclaiming agency over the body's alarm without expecting immediate perfection. You will learn to distinguish genuine signals from phantom threats, understand why suppression often amplifies sensations, and engage strategically with your physiology rather than avoiding it. The goal is not to conquer the body but to establish a more accurate dialogue, one where signals inform rather than terrify. In doing so, you dismantle the cycle that transforms fleeting fear into spiralling panic.

Prediction Error 101 – How the Brain's False Alarms Fuel Panic

One of the most disorienting aspects of anxiety is how convincingly real it feels in the body, even when logic insists there is no genuine threat. The pounding heart, the sudden rush of adrenaline, the hollow drop in the stomach—these sensations can arrive so suddenly, and with such intensity, that they seem to bypass rational analysis altogether. This is no coincidence. The brain's threat detection system is designed to prioritise speed over accuracy. It is far safer, evolutionarily speaking, to jump away from a stick mistaken for a snake than to pause for analysis and discover too late that the threat was real. This built-in bias towards false positives—what neuroscientists refer to as *prediction error*—is one of the key mechanisms behind panic and chronic anxiety.

At its core, prediction error is the gap between what the brain *expects* to happen and what is actually occurring. Our nervous system is not a passive recorder of events; it is a prediction machine, constantly forecasting the immediate future based on patterns it has learned. This predictive coding is highly efficient in stable environments—it allows us to walk without looking at our feet, catch a ball mid-flight, or speak fluently without consciously planning each word. But when this system becomes hypervigilant or biased towards danger, its forecasts skew sharply towards catastrophic interpretations. A sudden noise becomes an assumed threat. A skipped heartbeat becomes a sign of an impending medical emergency. A minor mistake at work becomes the precursor to career collapse. The error lies not in the body's ability to respond, but in the faulty prediction that triggered the response in the first place.

The amygdala, often described as the brain's alarm bell, is central to this process. It works in milliseconds, scanning sensory input for potential danger and issuing an immediate "prepare to act" signal to the rest of the body. It does this long before the prefrontal cortex—the brain's more analytical, reasoning centre—has time to evaluate the situation. This rapidity is a survival feature; in a genuine emergency, hesitation can be fatal. But when the amygdala's threshold for triggering is set too low, or when it has been trained by repeated anxious episodes, it can start treating ambiguous or benign stimuli as if they were genuinely life-threatening. The body reacts accordingly, and the physical sensations it generates often reinforce the original false prediction.

Consider the case of panic disorder. A person experiences a harmless but noticeable bodily change—perhaps their heart rate increases slightly after climbing stairs. The brain's prediction system, primed by past episodes of anxiety, interprets this as a precursor to another panic attack. The amygdala responds by triggering a full fight-or-flight cascade: adrenaline floods the bloodstream, breathing becomes rapid, and muscles tense in preparation for action. The person now feels *proof* that something terrible is happening, when in fact their body is simply responding to a misinterpreted signal. This loop can escalate rapidly, with each new wave of sensation reinforcing the original faulty prediction, creating what feels like a self-fulfilling crisis.

The challenge in breaking this loop lies in recognising that the sensations themselves are not the threat—they are the *result* of a mistaken prediction. This distinction is subtle but profound. Many people attempt to reassure themselves with rational arguments during a panic episode ("I am safe, this is just anxiety"), yet the body continues to react as if danger were imminent. This is because reassurance often addresses the *content* of the thought, not the predictive process that generated the alarm. If the brain's pattern recognition system still expects catastrophe, the body will still prepare for it.

Research into predictive coding shows that the brain is constantly comparing incoming sensory data with its expectations, adjusting either the prediction or the sensory weighting depending on the perceived mismatch. In anxiety, the brain often resolves the mismatch in favour of the prediction, discounting contradictory evidence. In other words, if you expect danger, you are more likely to interpret ambiguous signals as confirming it, even when the data points to safety. This bias can be self-reinforcing: each false alarm strengthens the network of associations between certain sensations and danger, making it more likely that similar sensations will trigger the same alarm in future.

Interestingly, prediction error is not inherently a flaw—it is the very mechanism by which we learn from experience. When the brain's predictions are wrong in a *helpful* direction—such as discovering that a feared event did not occur—it can update its model of the world and reduce unnecessary alarms. However, this updating requires not just cognitive awareness but repeated experiences of safety in the presence of the feared trigger. This is why exposure-based therapies can be so effective; they provide structured opportunities for the brain to collect accurate data, gradually recalibrating its predictions to match reality.

From a Stoic perspective, prediction error is another form of misjudgement—a premature and exaggerated assessment of a situation's significance. The ancient Stoics emphasised the importance of distinguishing between what is under our control and what is not. In the case of anxiety, we may not be able to prevent the amygdala from firing its false alarms, but we can influence how we respond to them. By recognising the pattern for what it is—a well-intentioned but misinformed survival reflex—we can reduce the secondary wave of fear that comes from believing the alarm must be accurate.

Modern examples abound. An executive preparing for a presentation might feel a rush of adrenaline moments before speaking and assume they are "losing control." A student taking an exam might interpret a momentary mental blank as proof of impending failure. In both cases, the brain's prediction—that physiological arousal equals catastrophe—fuels a stronger physical response, which in turn appears to confirm the prediction. Without an understanding of prediction error, these individuals are likely to misattribute their sensations to the wrong cause, reinforcing the anxiety cycle.

The way forward is not to eliminate prediction error—an impossible task—but to train the brain to tolerate and investigate it. This involves cultivating a stance of curiosity towards bodily sensations, recognising them as data rather than commands. It also means deliberately seeking experiences that disconfirm the anxious prediction, even in small ways. If the body predicts collapse when your heart rate increases, you might safely elevate it through brief exercise and observe the outcome. If the mind predicts humiliation in a social setting, you might experiment with low-stakes interactions and note the actual results. Over time, these experiences give the brain new reference points, making its predictions more accurate and less catastrophically skewed.

Ultimately, prediction error is not an enemy to be fought but a process to be understood and retrained. By appreciating that the body's false alarms are the product of an overzealous but well-meaning survival mechanism, we create space for a more measured response. The sensations lose some of their authority, the panic loop weakens, and the brain learns—slowly but reliably—that not every unexpected signal heralds disaster. In that recalibration lies the quiet but transformative shift from being at the mercy of the body's alarm system to being an informed interpreter of its messages.

Reset Routines – Quick Physiological Shifts to Dampen Runaway Fight-or-Flight Responses

The fight-or-flight response is one of the most powerful survival mechanisms humans possess, yet it is also one of the most easily misdirected. In situations of real danger, its rapid activation—flooding the body with adrenaline, increasing heart rate, sharpening sensory focus—can mean the difference between safety and harm. But when it fires in response to modern stressors such as a difficult conversation, a looming deadline, or an ambiguous email, the same changes that once ensured survival can become a source of distress. Left unchecked, the activation can escalate into what feels like a runaway physiological cascade, locking the body into a state of hyperarousal. Reset routines are designed to interrupt this escalation swiftly, not by arguing with anxious thoughts, but by working directly with the body's own systems to restore equilibrium.

One of the central challenges in managing acute stress is that the fight-or-flight system is largely automatic. Once the sympathetic nervous system surges, it can take minutes—or, in some cases, hours—for the body to return to baseline if left alone. The purpose of a reset routine is to *short-circuit this default trajectory*, using targeted physical interventions to send a clear "all clear" signal back to the brain. This works because the brain and body are in constant dialogue: if the brain perceives a threat, it mobilises the body for action; if the body signals calm, the brain updates its assessment accordingly. By engaging in deliberate, controlled actions that mimic the physiology of safety, we can exploit this feedback loop to reduce unnecessary arousal.

Consider the principle of respiratory control. Under threat, breathing tends to become shallow and rapid—an efficient way to oxygenate muscles quickly for action but an equally efficient way to increase sensations of panic when no physical threat exists. Controlled breathing techniques, such as slow diaphragmatic breathing or extended exhalation, work by directly stimulating the vagus nerve, which in turn activates the parasympathetic branch of the autonomic nervous system. This is not a vague relaxation exercise but a physiological intervention, shifting the body from a mobilisation state towards rest-and-digest. A pattern as simple as inhaling for four seconds, exhaling for six, repeated for several minutes, can measurably lower heart rate variability and bring the body closer to baseline.

Temperature change is another potent reset signal. The dive reflex—a primal response activated when the face is submerged in cold water—slows the heart rate and reduces blood pressure, conserving oxygen. Splashing cold water on the face, holding an ice pack against the cheeks, or immersing the face in a bowl of cold water can rapidly engage this reflex. While such actions might seem abrupt, they work precisely because they interrupt the body's escalating stress signals with a competing and non-threatening physiological demand. Professional free divers use this reflex to extend breath-hold times, but in the context of anxiety, it becomes a tool for halting runaway sympathetic activation.

Muscular tension and release also play a critical role in resetting the body. Under stress, large muscle groups tense involuntarily, priming the body for movement. This tension, if unaddressed, becomes a constant signal to the brain that danger is present. Progressive muscle relaxation—deliberately contracting a muscle group for several seconds before releasing it—provides contrasting feedback, signalling that voluntary control is intact and immediate threat has passed. In practice, this might mean clenching the fists tightly for five seconds before letting them soften, or pressing the feet firmly into the floor before releasing. The movement from tension to release reinforces a sense of control and offers the brain an updated sensory map that no longer aligns with imminent danger.

Movement itself is another underutilised but highly effective reset. In the evolutionary context, fleeing from or fighting a threat discharged the physiological activation generated by the stress response. In modern contexts, we often experience the activation without the physical outlet—sitting at a desk, trapped in a meeting, or scrolling on a phone while the body prepares for action it never takes. Brief bursts of controlled movement—walking briskly, performing short sets of bodyweight exercises, even shaking out the limbs—can help metabolise the adrenaline and cortisol that the stress response has released. This is not about "burning off" anxiety through exhaustive exercise, but about completing the incomplete stress cycle so that the body can return to a resting state.

The effectiveness of reset routines lies not only in their mechanics but also in their *speed*. When the stress response is intercepted early, before it has fully escalated, it is easier to redirect. This means cultivating awareness of early warning signs: the first quickened breath, the slight increase in heart rate, the narrowing of focus. By acting at this threshold, rather than waiting until panic or agitation has peaked, the routines require less effort and produce quicker relief. In this sense, reset routines are less about "fixing" a full-blown episode and more about *preventing escalation.*

A potential counterpoint is that relying on such interventions could become a form of avoidance, where the person uses them to suppress discomfort rather than address the underlying trigger. This is where intentional use becomes crucial. Reset routines are not meant to replace cognitive or behavioural work on the root causes of anxiety; rather, they create the physiological stability needed to approach those causes without being overwhelmed. They give the individual enough breathing room—literally and figuratively—to respond thoughtfully instead of reacting impulsively.

Modern applications of reset routines are broad. Elite athletes use them to maintain composure before high-stakes performances, surgeons to steady hands before complex procedures, negotiators to sustain clarity in tense discussions. In each case, the physiological mechanism is the same: the body is cued to downshift from a mobilised state into a state of readiness without overactivation. Even in day-to-day contexts, such as preparing to speak in a meeting or responding to a challenging email, these techniques can prevent the fight-or-flight response from hijacking decision-making capacity.

For those who wish to integrate reset routines into their lives, consistency matters. A single exposure may help in the moment, but repeated practice embeds the techniques into muscle memory, making them easier to deploy under pressure. Just as a fire drill trains the body to respond efficiently in an emergency, rehearsing reset routines when calm ensures they are accessible when it counts. This is especially important because the higher the arousal, the harder it becomes to recall and implement new strategies.

Ultimately, the value of reset routines lies in their capacity to return agency to the individual in moments when the body seems to have seized control. They work not by denying the reality of the stress response but by engaging with it on its own terms—through breath, temperature, movement, and muscle control—offering the brain fresh data that contradicts the urgency of the alarm. In doing so, they do more than provide momentary relief; they lay the groundwork for a recalibrated nervous system, one that can distinguish more accurately between genuine threats and modern-day false alarms. This recalibration is the quiet but decisive step from being carried away by the body's reflexes to steering them with deliberate intent.

Interoceptive Exposure – Guided Exercises to Safely Feel and Accept Bodily Sensations of Anxiety

The body's alarm system is often less frightening than the meaning we attach to it. A racing heart, lightheadedness, or shortness of breath are not inherently dangerous—yet for those caught in the grip of anxiety, these sensations can feel like harbingers of collapse, madness, or loss of control. The problem is not merely the sensations themselves but the conditioned reflex to treat them as threats. Interoceptive exposure is designed to dismantle that reflex. By deliberately evoking and staying with the bodily sensations of anxiety in a controlled setting, it retrains the nervous system to interpret them as tolerable, even unremarkable. In doing so, it undercuts one of anxiety's most persistent feedback loops: *the fear of fear itself.*

Many anxiety disorders, especially panic disorder, are maintained by what psychologists term "catastrophic misinterpretation" of bodily cues. A slight elevation in heart rate is read as "I'm about to have a heart attack"; a momentary sense of unreality becomes "I'm going to lose my mind." This interpretation triggers further sympathetic activation, which in turn amplifies the sensations, seemingly confirming the fear. It is a self-reinforcing spiral. Traditional avoidance—avoiding exercise to prevent heart palpitations, steering clear of hot rooms to avoid sweating—might offer short-term relief, but it reinforces the association between sensation and danger, ensuring the cycle remains intact. Interoceptive exposure breaks this cycle by replacing avoidance with intentional, repeated confrontation.

The method's power lies in its precision. It targets the bodily sensations themselves, not just the situations in which they occur. If dizziness is a trigger, the exercise might involve spinning in a chair; if shortness of breath provokes fear, the person might breathe through a straw for a set period. The aim is not to "provoke an attack" but to normalise the experience of these sensations so that they no longer automatically signal danger. Through repeated exposure, the brain learns a new association: these sensations are uncomfortable but harmless. The amygdala—the brain's threat detection centre—gradually reduces its overreaction, much like how a fire alarm stops going off when the toast burns but no fire follows.

A typical interoceptive exposure programme is both structured and progressive. It begins with less intense sensations and gradually builds toward those that are most feared. This is not about shock tactics; it is about calibrated learning. The exercises are chosen with clear rationale, and each is followed by a period of observation, allowing the participant to notice that the feared outcome did not occur. Over time, *habituation*—a natural decrease in emotional and physiological response—emerges. In parallel, *inhibitory learning* takes place: the brain retains the original fear association but overlays it with a stronger, more accurate one. In effect, the fear memory is not erased but rendered irrelevant.

The counterintuitive aspect of interoceptive exposure is that it invites the very sensations people have spent years avoiding. This can provoke scepticism, even resistance. It is worth acknowledging that avoidance often develops from a place of logic: if something feels dangerous, staying away from it seems wise. Yet in the case of anxiety sensations, avoidance is akin to avoiding the sight of your own shadow—it offers temporary relief but ultimately magnifies the fear. The courage to turn towards these sensations, to elicit them on purpose, is both the risk and the reward of the method.

Clinical research consistently supports its efficacy. Studies of panic disorder have shown that interoceptive exposure, particularly when combined with cognitive restructuring, significantly reduces both the frequency and intensity of panic attacks. Its effects are durable because the learning is embodied; the individual does not merely "know" intellectually that the sensations are safe, they have felt them repeatedly in safety, dissolving the urgency at its root. This distinction between intellectual reassurance and experiential learning is crucial. The body learns in a way that words alone cannot teach.

Interoceptive exposure also has broader applications beyond panic disorder. In health anxiety, it can help disentangle benign bodily fluctuations from catastrophic interpretations. In social anxiety, it can reduce fear of blushing, trembling, or sweating in public. Even athletes and performers can use the method to become comfortable with the adrenaline surges that accompany competition or stage presence, preventing those sensations from tipping into panic. The universality of the principle—safe exposure to feared bodily cues—makes it a versatile tool across contexts.

Still, the method is not without challenges. Some individuals may find that sensations evoke memories of past trauma, making the experience more complex than straightforward habituation. For these cases, exposure needs to be adapted, perhaps integrated into a broader therapeutic approach that includes grounding and self-regulation skills. Others may push too quickly, mistaking intensity for progress, only to retraumatise themselves. The pacing of interoceptive exposure is therefore as important as its content; success comes not from overwhelming the nervous system but from steadily proving to it that the alarm is false.

One of the subtler benefits of interoceptive exposure is the shift in self-concept it fosters. People often describe feeling "fragile" or "at the mercy" of their anxiety before undertaking the exercises. After repeated, controlled encounters with feared sensations, that identity begins to change. They move from "I can't handle this" to "I have felt this before and I know I can tolerate it." This is not bravado; it is earned confidence, grounded in lived evidence. It changes the way one relates to future episodes of arousal—not as crises to be averted, but as temporary states that can be navigated.

The Stoic resonance here is unmistakable. The Stoics trained themselves to meet adversity without flinching, often by rehearsing discomfort in advance. Seneca wrote of "practising poverty" to remove the sting of deprivation should it come. Interoceptive exposure is a modern analogue for this principle, applying it to the internal landscape of bodily sensation. By feeling in advance what we fear to feel, we strip the fear of its power. The sensations remain, but their narrative changes; they are no longer omens of disaster, merely passing waves in the body's ongoing dialogue with the mind.

Ultimately, interoceptive exposure is an exercise in truth-testing. It dismantles the false equation of bodily arousal with imminent catastrophe and replaces it with a more accurate, lived understanding. It is neither denial nor suppression—it is the deliberate act of looking the body's alarm in the eye and discovering that it blinks first. And in that discovery, one gains not only freedom from the fear of sensation but a deeper trust in one's capacity to remain steady in the midst of it.

Physical Recovery Windows – Teaches Rest Phases to Prevent Sensitisation of the Nervous System

The nervous system is not designed to run at maximum alert indefinitely. Like any high-performance engine, it requires cool-down periods to prevent damage and maintain efficiency. Yet modern life—and particularly the experience of chronic anxiety—often deprives it of these essential rest phases. When the sympathetic nervous system is triggered repeatedly without adequate recovery, it becomes increasingly sensitised. This means that smaller and smaller stimuli can provoke disproportionate responses, as if the alarm system has been recalibrated to detect threat everywhere. Over time, this heightened reactivity can make a person feel trapped in a perpetual state of tension, where even minor stressors tip them into fight-or-flight mode. Physical recovery windows are not indulgences; they are the physiological reset mechanisms that protect against this downward spiral.

Sensitisation is not purely psychological. It is a neurobiological process involving changes in both the brain and the peripheral nervous system. Prolonged or repeated activation of stress pathways increases baseline cortisol levels, alters the responsiveness of the amygdala, and shifts the body's set point toward hypervigilance. In this state, the threshold for triggering an adrenaline surge is dramatically reduced. A missed email, an unexpected phone call, or a change in routine can provoke the same intensity of response that would once have been reserved for genuine emergencies. Rest phases reverse this drift. They allow the parasympathetic nervous system to reassert its influence, recalibrating the body's balance between arousal and recovery. This is not merely "feeling relaxed"; it is the neurochemical process of restoring resilience.

One of the reasons recovery windows are often neglected is that the early warning signs of sensitisation can be subtle. People may notice they are more irritable, have trouble concentrating, or experience fragmented sleep. Physical symptoms such as muscle tightness, headaches, or gastrointestinal discomfort can also creep in. These are not random ailments—they are the body's way of signalling that the load is unsustainable. Without deliberate recovery periods, these signs accumulate into chronic states such as generalised anxiety, panic disorder, or burnout. The mind may rationalise pushing through, but the body keeps score.

In practice, physical recovery windows can take many forms, but their effectiveness hinges on their capacity to shift the body's physiological state, not simply to distract the mind. Scrolling through a phone or watching high-intensity television is not recovery; the sympathetic system remains subtly engaged. True recovery triggers parasympathetic dominance—lowered heart rate, deeper breathing, muscle relaxation, and improved digestion. This can be achieved through low-intensity movement such as walking outdoors, diaphragmatic breathing, gentle stretching, or even deliberate stillness. Short, structured naps have been shown to improve cardiovascular regulation, while exposure to natural environments can measurably reduce cortisol within minutes. The common factor is that these practices give the nervous system the unambiguous signal that danger has passed.

From a performance perspective—whether in athletics, public speaking, or high-pressure professional environments—recovery windows are not downtime, they are an integral component of sustained output. Elite athletes structure rest into their training cycles with the same precision they apply to workouts, recognising that without it, gains cannot consolidate. The same principle applies to psychological endurance. Without intervals of nervous system recovery, the capacity to tolerate stress contracts, making once-manageable challenges feel overwhelming.

There is a deeper cognitive dimension to recovery as well. When arousal levels remain high, the brain's attentional system narrows toward threat detection. This constrains creativity, problem-solving, and long-term planning—capacities that require the wider perceptual bandwidth of a calmer state. Recovery periods re-expand this cognitive frame, making it possible to see options and connections that high arousal obscures. This is why solutions to intractable problems often emerge not during prolonged effort, but during a walk, a shower, or a moment of quiet reflection. Physiological recovery and cognitive flexibility are intertwined.

The Stoics understood this interplay long before neuroscience could map it. Marcus Aurelius frequently wrote about retreating into himself—not to escape life, but to return to it with steadier judgment. These were not days-long withdrawals but brief, deliberate intervals in which he allowed his mind to detach from immediate pressures and reconnect with guiding principles. The modern equivalent need not be cloistered solitude; it can be a disciplined practice of micro-breaks throughout the day. Two minutes of slow breathing between meetings, ten minutes of sunlight in the morning, a short walk after lunch—each of these is a recovery window that, when consistently applied, raises the baseline of nervous system stability.

It is important to distinguish recovery from avoidance. The goal is not to retreat from every source of discomfort, but to cycle between adaptive challenge and adequate restoration. Just as muscles grow stronger through the alternation of exertion and rest, the nervous system becomes more resilient through the alternation of activation and calm. The risk of neglecting recovery is not only increased anxiety but eventual collapse into exhaustion, where even small demands become unmanageable. The risk of overusing recovery, on the other hand, is stagnation—a life oriented around minimising all arousal. The skill lies in striking the balance, ensuring that recovery serves performance rather than replaces it.

Incorporating recovery windows into daily life requires intentionality because the default of modern culture is continuous engagement. Devices keep the nervous system tethered to alerts, notifications, and the low-level uncertainty of "what's next?" The absence of obvious danger does not equate to rest; in fact, the chronic partial attention this creates is itself a form of mild arousal. Scheduling recovery—whether through structured breaks, defined cut-off times for work, or technology-free intervals—reclaims the body's right to stand down. Over time, this deliberate disengagement reconditions the stress response, making the nervous system less likely to overreact.

Perhaps the most compelling argument for physical recovery windows is that they compound over time. A single moment of deep breathing may feel insignificant, but repeated daily over months it can shift the body's baseline from high alert to balanced readiness. This cumulative effect is not easily perceived in the moment, which is why people often abandon recovery practices too soon. The nervous system learns through repetition; every intentional rest period reinforces the association between safety and these specific cues, making calm states more accessible in future.

In essence, physical recovery windows are the nervous system's maintenance schedule. They do not remove life's pressures, but they ensure the machinery is kept in working order to handle them. They protect against the corrosive effect of unrelieved activation, preserve the capacity for clear thought under stress, and extend the range of challenges a person can meet without becoming overwhelmed. By treating recovery as a strategic necessity rather than an optional luxury, one not only prevents sensitisation but actively builds the foundation for long-term resilience.

Chapter 8
Social Anxiety Without Scripts

For many intelligent and capable individuals, social anxiety is not rooted in ignorance of what to say or do, but in the oppressive weight of how they believe they must appear. This is not shyness in the sense of being tongue-tied or socially inexperienced; it is the tension of an internal performance standard set to impossible heights. The idea that acceptance depends on perfect composure, flawless delivery, and the absence of visible nerves is a seductive illusion—one reinforced by curated online personas, polished public speakers, and the selective memory of our own best social moments. Yet this myth of perfect presence creates the very fragility it seeks to avoid. In reality, people are drawn to others not for their errorless presentation but for the authenticity that survives, and sometimes thrives, in the presence of imperfection. To believe otherwise is to step into every interaction already primed for threat detection rather than connection.

The nervous system treats social exposure as a form of uncertainty. For our evolutionary ancestors, acceptance by the group was a survival imperative, and exclusion could be fatal. That ancient circuitry still operates, but modern environments amplify it with constant opportunities for self-comparison and imagined judgement. Under social anxiety, even trivial interactions can feel like high-stakes trials, as though every pause in conversation or ambiguous glance confirms one's worst fears about how they are perceived. In this state, the mind does not experience the present moment as it is, but as a continuous scan for evidence of rejection. This vigilance, far from improving performance, degrades it—eroding spontaneity, shrinking attention, and filtering every word through the lens of risk.

To manage this threat, many people adopt safety behaviours. These are subtle but deliberate strategies to minimise perceived exposure: rehearsing sentences before speaking, avoiding eye contact to prevent scrutiny, speaking only in safe topics, or withdrawing entirely from unpredictable settings. While such measures can give a temporary sense of control, they are corrosive over time. Each one reinforces the belief that without them, social disaster is inevitable. The avoidance is self-confirming: by never testing whether you can survive without the crutch, you never disprove the fear. This is why safety behaviours are not merely neutral habits—they are a form of low-grade self-imprisonment.

The alternative is not to leap without preparation into the most intimidating scenarios, but to introduce *micro-risks*—small, deliberate steps that disrupt the belief that every deviation from a perfect script leads to humiliation. This might mean initiating a brief conversation without rehearsing, holding eye contact for a moment longer than is comfortable, or offering a candid opinion rather than a safe agreement. Each of these acts, while seemingly minor, challenges the nervous system's prediction of catastrophe. Over time, they build a lived track record that fear is not an accurate oracle. This is where the craft of change lies: in shifting the internal cost–benefit calculation until risk-taking is no longer synonymous with loss.

The Stoics offer a perspective that reframes social exposure altogether. For thinkers like Epictetus and Marcus Aurelius, the opinions of others—though impossible to control—should be placed firmly outside the boundary of what determines our self-worth. This is not a call to arrogance or emotional withdrawal; Stoic detachment is not the cold dismissal of human connection. Rather, it is the recognition that while another's reaction may be valuable information, it is not an ultimate verdict on one's character. A raised eyebrow, a disinterested tone, or even open criticism need not be internalised as proof of inadequacy. By loosening the grip of other people's imagined evaluations, one regains the capacity to act in alignment with personal values rather than under the coercion of projected judgement.

In the context of social anxiety, this detachment is liberating because it shifts the role of the other person from judge to participant. The conversation ceases to be a performance for approval and becomes a shared activity whose outcome is influenced, but not defined, by your own contribution. This reframing makes it possible to engage without the constant calculation of "how am I doing?" and to accept that the discomfort of uncertainty is not a flaw in the process but an inherent part of authentic human exchange. Ironically, it is often when we abandon the script that we come closest to the connection we have been trying to engineer.

This chapter dismantles the false logic that fuels socially anxious behaviour and replaces it with principles that can be practised in real time. By confronting the myth of perfect presence, shedding the protective armour of safety behaviours, and taking controlled social risks, it becomes possible to move through conversation without the constant burden of self-monitoring. Layered over this is the Stoic capacity to engage fully without handing over the keys of self-worth to the fluctuating opinions of others. The aim is not to become immune to discomfort, but to recalibrate one's relationship with it—until the nervous system recognises that social uncertainty is survivable, and connection is possible without control.

The Myth of Perfect Presence – Debunks the belief that flawless performance is required for acceptance

One of the most persistent and quietly damaging beliefs in socially anxious minds is that there exists such a thing as *perfect presence*—a manner of being in which every word is eloquent, every gesture well-timed, every response effortlessly apt, and every silence gracefully poised. The fantasy is seductive because it seems to promise immunity from rejection: if I can perform without flaw, I will be accepted without question. But this idea is not merely unrealistic; it is actively harmful. It sets an unattainable standard against which all social encounters are measured and inevitably found wanting, fuelling self-criticism before, during, and after interactions. The irony is that the pursuit of perfect presence erodes the very qualities—ease, attentiveness, emotional connection—that make people compelling in the first place.

Part of the problem is that perfection, in social contexts, is defined retroactively. When recalling an exchange, we selectively highlight our supposed missteps—a slightly awkward pause, a word choice that now feels imprecise, a laugh that landed too loudly or too softly—and judge the entire encounter by these moments. Yet we do not apply this forensic scrutiny to others. A friend's mispronunciation or a colleague's lapse in phrasing is rarely remembered beyond the instant. Social perfection, then, is not a universal expectation; it is a personal fiction applied only to oneself, maintained through confirmation bias and an internalised belief that one is uniquely visible and judged.

The pressure to sustain this illusion is compounded by the cultural environments many of us inhabit. Digital communication, with its capacity for editing, filtering, and rehearsing, creates a skewed baseline for human interaction. On social media, moments are curated for maximum wit, relevance, and visual appeal; in professional spheres, presentations and public appearances are often the result of multiple rehearsals and post-production polish. The unfiltered, messy reality of in-person conversation does not stand a chance against these artefacts of selective presentation. This mismatch fosters the quiet suspicion that others are operating effortlessly at the same level of polish we see online, making our own perceived imperfections feel glaring by comparison.

Yet research into social connection suggests that perfection is not only unnecessary for acceptance—it can actually be detrimental. Studies on the "pratfall effect" have shown that competent individuals who display small, humanising mistakes are often liked more than those who appear flawless. The imperfection signals approachability; it communicates that the other person is not an untouchable ideal but someone relatable, fallible, and therefore safe to engage with. In practice, many of our warmest connections are forged not in the moments we present our best rehearsed selves, but when we accidentally reveal something unscripted—when we laugh too hard, admit uncertainty, or momentarily lose our train of thought. These moments invite reciprocity rather than competition.

The belief in perfect presence is sustained by a false equivalence between performance and worth. This is particularly evident in high-pressure professions where visibility is constant and errors can have real consequences—lawyers in courtrooms, physicians delivering difficult news, executives in boardrooms. In such arenas, the stakes for precision are genuine, but the assumption that *every* social interaction requires the same meticulous standard is misguided. Treating casual conversation like a high-stakes negotiation not only exhausts the mind but also narrows one's expressive range, reducing spontaneity and adaptability. The more a person rehearses and self-monitors, the more they are pulled into a closed feedback loop in which their focus shifts away from the shared moment and onto their own performance metrics.

The paradox here is that the traits most associated with "good presence"—authenticity, attentiveness, and responsiveness—cannot be manufactured under constant self-surveillance. They emerge when the mind is oriented outward, engaged with the other person and the context rather than with an internal scorecard. This does not mean abandoning social skill or self-awareness, but rather recognising that the pursuit of flawless execution is counterproductive. The aim should be coherence and connection, not perfection. A speaker who occasionally hesitates while finding the right word can still command a room if their overall message resonates and their presence feels genuine.

Philosophically, this shift requires dismantling the idea that acceptance is granted only to those who meet a pre-existing ideal. The Stoics would remind us that the opinions of others are outside our control and therefore cannot be the measure of our worth. By that logic, the belief that one can "earn" universal acceptance through perfect performance is not only irrational but self-defeating: it ties one's peace of mind to a variable that is inherently unstable. This perspective reframes social interaction as a space for contribution, not judgement—a collaborative act in which imperfection is inevitable and often inconsequential.

Pragmatically, loosening the grip of this belief can be approached through deliberate experiments. Allowing oneself to speak without rehearsing every word, resisting the urge to fill every silence, or admitting "I don't know" in response to a question can be small but potent acts of rebellion against the myth. The purpose is not to cultivate sloppiness but to gather experiential evidence that social approval is not contingent on a flawless performance. Over time, these acts recalibrate the nervous system's expectation of danger and replace it with a more realistic sense of resilience.

To abandon the myth of perfect presence is to replace a life of constant auditioning with one of genuine participation. It is an invitation to shift from *how am I doing?* to *what is happening between us?*—

from self-monitoring to shared attention. This change does not remove all anxiety, nor should it aim to; some degree of alertness is natural in situations that matter to us. But it does free the mind from the exhausting and futile task of striving for a standard that no human interaction has ever truly required. In its place comes a more sustainable, more humane metric for social success: not the absence of mistakes, but the presence of connection.

Dropping Safety Behaviours – Shows how over-preparing or avoiding eye contact actually reinforces fear

The paradox of social anxiety is that the very strategies designed to prevent humiliation often ensure that the fear never fades. These strategies—known as *safety behaviours*—are subtle acts of self-protection deployed in the hope of avoiding negative judgement. They can be as visible as avoiding eye contact or as covert as rehearsing every sentence before speaking. They feel sensible, even necessary, in the moment. Yet the evidence from decades of psychological research is clear: safety behaviours protect the anxiety, not the person. They prevent the mind from learning the crucial lesson that feared outcomes are rare, survivable, and often imagined. By cushioning the self from perceived threat, they inadvertently confirm that the threat is real.

Consider the student who never speaks in seminars without having scripted their contribution in advance. The plan seems to guarantee competence, but it also guarantees that the student never experiences the alternative—that spontaneous speaking might go well enough without meticulous rehearsal. Each successful interaction is attributed not to their ability but to the presence of the script. The same principle applies to the employee who avoids eye contact in meetings to evade the possibility of scrutiny; the relief they feel reinforces the belief that being seen is dangerous, ensuring the cycle repeats. Safety behaviours keep anxiety on life support by removing opportunities for corrective experience.

The difficulty is that safety behaviours are not always obvious. To the person using them, they often feel like rational preparation or simple politeness. Carrying a glass of water at all times might be framed as a harmless habit, yet for someone who fears blushing or trembling, it can function as a prop—a way to mask physical symptoms and to buy time in conversation. Standing near the exit during a crowded event can feel like strategic positioning, but it also signals to the nervous system that escape is necessary. These micro-choices accumulate into a subtle architecture of avoidance, narrowing the range of what feels safe.

Behavioural experiments in clinical settings have repeatedly shown the value of reducing or dropping safety behaviours entirely. When individuals are encouraged to face anxiety-provoking situations without their protective habits, the initial discomfort often spikes. But in the absence of the safety net, something important happens: the feared outcome either fails to materialise or, if it does, proves far less catastrophic than expected. A classic study by Salkovskis and colleagues demonstrated that socially anxious participants who deliberately refrained from using their usual safety behaviours—such as planning sentences in advance or holding objects to mask shaking—reported not only less anxiety over time but also more positive reactions from others. Without the distraction of self-monitoring and compensatory tactics, they engaged more naturally.

The principle here is not masochistic; it is empirical. The brain learns through exposure and feedback. Safety behaviours distort this process by altering the conditions of exposure, making it impossible to determine whether the feared situation is genuinely unsafe or whether the safety measure was unnecessary. Dropping them restores the integrity of the experiment: it allows the mind to experience unfiltered reality. This is a profoundly Stoic move—not because the Stoics were concerned with eye contact per se, but because they understood the futility of expending energy on what lies outside our control. In social contexts, others' reactions cannot be perfectly managed, and efforts to do so often erode authenticity.

Of course, abandoning safety behaviours cannot be done wholesale for everyone at once; the nervous system resists sudden exposure to unmitigated fear. A more effective approach is to identify one or two safety behaviours and test their absence in low-stakes scenarios. For instance, a person who habitually avoids speaking up in group settings might choose to contribute a single unrehearsed comment in a meeting where the consequences are minimal. The aim is not to perform flawlessly but to observe whether the feared outcome occurs and, if so, whether it is tolerable. Repeated trials of this kind recalibrate the body's alarm system, replacing learned associations of danger with evidence of resilience.

One reason safety behaviours are so sticky is that they produce immediate relief. The moment the socially anxious individual avoids eye contact, the sharp spike of self-consciousness subsides. This relief, however, is the engine of long-term maintenance—it strengthens the association between avoidance and safety. Breaking this cycle requires tolerating short-term discomfort in service of long-term freedom. Here, physiological self-regulation techniques—steady breathing, grounding through sensory awareness—can support the experiment by keeping the anxiety at a manageable level while the safety behaviour is withheld.

Critically, dropping safety behaviours is not about stripping away all preparation or politeness from social interaction. It is about distinguishing between what serves genuine connection and what serves only to shield the self from imagined harm. Preparing for a lecture because one wishes to communicate clearly is different from scripting every sentence out of fear of blanking; maintaining appropriate gaze to convey interest is different from locking eyes in an attempt to project dominance. The former choices expand one's range, the latter constrict it. The task is to notice the difference and to progressively discard those habits whose primary function is fear management.

The counterintuitive truth is that others often respond more favourably when we drop safety behaviours, because these behaviours, while meant to hide anxiety, can inadvertently create social distance. Avoiding eye contact can read as disinterest; over-rehearsed speech can sound inauthentic; keeping one's hands perpetually occupied can make one seem disengaged. When these are removed, the individual may appear more open, responsive, and relatable—even if they still feel anxious internally. Over time, the external feedback loop begins to work in their favour, gradually aligning their internal state with the more positive reality.

To dismantle safety behaviours is to return to a form of unarmoured engagement with the social world. It requires a certain philosophical courage: the willingness to be seen without guarantees, to risk small failures in order to dismantle the illusion of catastrophic outcomes. In this way, the work is less about forcing confidence than about cultivating tolerance for imperfection and unpredictability. By releasing the grip on these subtle defences, one allows for the possibility of genuine interaction—an exchange in which acceptance, if it comes, is not the reward for flawless performance, but the natural result of showing up as oneself.

Micro-Risks in Conversation – Encourages small, deliberate steps to test social fears

If social anxiety is maintained by avoidance, then the antidote is not a reckless leap into the most feared situation but a series of controlled incursions into discomfort. These *micro-risks* are the smallest meaningful steps that challenge the internal prediction of social catastrophe. They are not grand gestures or radical reinventions of one's social persona; rather, they are deliberate, bounded experiments designed to gather evidence about reality and dismantle the assumptions that keep anxiety entrenched. The genius of micro-risks is that they are too small to overwhelm yet large enough to disrupt the cycle of fear and avoidance.

The logic behind this approach mirrors principles from both cognitive behavioural therapy and exposure science. The socially anxious mind is often operating on outdated or exaggerated threat data—memories of past embarrassment, inherited beliefs about judgment, or over-amplified readings of bodily signals. By introducing a micro-risk into conversation, one tests these assumptions without triggering the kind of defensive shutdown that occurs when exposure is too intense. The process becomes iterative: act, observe, update. Over time, this recalibrates both expectation and tolerance.

Consider the example of someone who avoids disagreeing with colleagues for fear of seeming confrontational. A micro-risk might involve voicing a mild preference for one option over another in a low-stakes meeting. The purpose is not to win the argument but to observe whether others react with disdain or whether the feared fallout actually occurs. If the predicted negative reaction fails to materialise, the brain receives an update: disagreement does not automatically equal social rejection. If mild pushback does occur, the individual has an opportunity to test their ability to tolerate it without retreating into avoidance. Either outcome generates useful data.

Micro-risks can be tailored with remarkable precision. For someone who fears prolonged eye contact, the step might be maintaining gaze for two or three seconds longer than usual in a single conversation, then noting the other person's reaction. For someone who hides behind overly formal language, the experiment might involve introducing one casual remark in a professional context to test whether rapport improves or declines. The parameters matter: too small and the brain dismisses the experience as irrelevant; too large and the resulting anxiety may confirm the original fear. The art lies in finding the edge of one's comfort zone and stepping just beyond it.

Importantly, micro-risks are not about adopting a different personality or forcing extroversion. They are about removing self-imposed constraints that limit authentic expression. The socially anxious person often operates within a set of invisible rules—*never initiate conversation unless certain of interest, avoid talking about yourself unless asked directly, stick to safe topics*. Micro-risks loosen these rules through targeted, low-stakes breaches. The aim is not to abandon all social norms but to test whether these rigid personal codes are necessary or simply habitual.

Research on graded exposure supports the cumulative effect of such interventions. Small, repeated challenges, when carried out consistently, lead to measurable reductions in anxiety responses. This is because each micro-risk creates a mini "violation" of the brain's expectation, resulting in a *prediction error*—a mismatch between anticipated threat and actual outcome. Neuroscience has shown that these moments of discrepancy are powerful learning opportunities. The amygdala's threat signalling begins to quiet, and the prefrontal cortex gains more influence over the interpretation of social cues.

There is also a philosophical dimension to micro-risks. They embody a Stoic principle: focus on what you can control—your willingness to act—rather than the reactions of others, which are beyond your command. By setting the challenge as "speak once in this meeting" rather than "impress everyone," the measure of success shifts from external validation to internal follow-through. This reframe reduces the emotional stakes, making it easier to act and harder for self-criticism to derail progress.

Micro-risks also have a social feedback function. Safety behaviours and avoidance tend to limit the quality of interactions, sometimes creating a self-fulfilling prophecy in which the anxious person appears distant or disengaged. Small risks—asking a personal question, sharing a brief story, offering an unpolished opinion—can invite reciprocity and deepen connection. This, in turn, produces reinforcing experiences that further erode the belief that social engagement is inherently perilous.

The strategic use of micro-risks requires tracking. Without conscious review, the lessons of these small experiments can be lost to the noise of daily life. Journalling outcomes—both the objective facts and the subjective feelings—helps anchor the learning. For instance, a note might read: *Maintained eye contact with client for full sentence. Felt anxious at first, but noticed they smiled. Anxiety dropped after 10 seconds.* Such records make progress visible and provide a counterweight to the distorted recall that anxiety often fuels, where one remembers only perceived failures and dismisses small wins.

There is a temptation to interpret micro-risks as mere warm-ups for "real" exposure—the ultimate goal being to tackle one's biggest fears head-on. While that can be true, their value is not limited to preparatory work. Micro-risks can become an ongoing maintenance strategy, a way of keeping social flexibility alive even after anxiety has diminished. Social contexts are dynamic; new environments, roles, or relationships can trigger old fears. Having a habit of small, deliberate challenges ensures that the skill of adaptive risk-taking remains active.

One of the most understated benefits of micro-risks is the shift in identity they foster. Each successful experiment, however modest, begins to chip away at the self-image of someone "unable to cope" with certain situations. The individual starts to see themselves as capable of entering uncertainty and navigating it competently. This identity shift is not built on dramatic transformations but on a steady accumulation of lived proof. By the time larger challenges are attempted, the foundation is already in place.

In practice, micro-risks are deceptively simple, but their power lies in repetition and reflection. They are the quiet, daily acts that gradually rewire a hypervigilant social brain. For the time-conscious professional, the researcher accustomed to intellectual but not interpersonal risk, or the student seeking confidence beyond rehearsed presentations, they offer a methodical, evidence-based path forward. And because they are small, they are sustainable—woven into the fabric of normal interaction rather than staged as special events. Over time, they transform conversation from a minefield to a landscape of navigable possibilities, not through force, but through a hundred small acts of deliberate courage.

Stoic Detachment in Social Contexts – Applies Stoic indifference to others' opinions without losing empathy

Few beliefs imprison the socially anxious more tightly than the conviction that their worth hinges on the opinions of others. The moment we grant strangers or acquaintances the authority to dictate our sense of self, every interaction becomes an evaluation and every silence a potential condemnation. The Stoics recognised this centuries ago. They argued that while we cannot control what others think, we can control the weight we assign to those judgments. This was not an invitation to rudeness or coldness; it was a call to reframe our relationship with approval so that it no longer governs our peace of mind.

At the heart of Stoic detachment lies the distinction between what is within our control and what is not. Marcus Aurelius, reflecting in his private writings, reminded himself that others' opinions belong to them, not to him. They are shaped by their own experiences, biases, and shifting emotional states—variables entirely beyond our influence. To be guided by them is to live as a perpetual hostage. Yet Stoic detachment is not synonymous with emotional withdrawal. To practise it effectively in social contexts requires holding two positions at once: caring enough to act with kindness and clarity, yet refusing to let another's appraisal determine one's inner equilibrium.

Modern psychology corroborates the Stoic view with research on self-determination theory and internal versus external loci of control. Individuals whose sense of worth is anchored internally tend to experience less stress in evaluative situations. Their actions are guided by personal values and self-chosen standards rather than by the fluctuating tides of public perception. Social confidence, in this model, does not come from being universally liked; it comes from knowing that one can face disapproval without being undone by it.

The challenge, however, is applying this principle in environments where approval genuinely has consequences—job interviews, client meetings, academic defences. Stoic detachment does not deny the strategic value of making a favourable impression in such contexts. It asks instead for a disciplined separation between effort and outcome: *I will prepare diligently and present clearly, but I will not equate rejection with personal inadequacy.* This distinction allows for full engagement in the task without the corrosive fear that every imperfect moment signals failure.

Empathy plays a vital role here. Detachment without empathy risks becoming callousness, alienating others and undermining social trust. Stoic empathy is not about emotional fusion—absorbing another's feelings as one's own—but about perspective-taking: recognising another person's humanity and responding accordingly, without surrendering one's emotional stability. In conversation, this means listening attentively and responding with thoughtfulness, but declining to let signs of boredom, irritation, or criticism dictate one's self-worth.

Consider the colleague who appears curt during your presentation. A reactive, approval-dependent mindset might spiral into self-doubt—*I'm failing; they dislike me.* A Stoic response would observe the behaviour, acknowledge it as their own mental state, and continue with clarity. Afterwards, one might investigate whether their reaction was due to disagreement, distraction, or personal stress, but without the assumption that it reflects a definitive judgment of one's competence. In doing so, the interaction becomes an exchange of information rather than a referendum on identity.

One reason Stoic detachment is difficult to maintain is the human brain's bias towards social threat detection. Evolutionarily, being ostracised from the group could mean reduced chances of survival, so our nervous systems are tuned to pick up on disapproval. Stoic training functions as a deliberate override of this reflex. By repeatedly exposing ourselves to moments of possible disapproval—voicing a dissenting opinion, maintaining a position politely in the face of pushback—we teach the nervous system that such experiences, while uncomfortable, are survivable.

Crucially, detachment is not passive indifference. It involves active discernment: weighing whether feedback aligns with one's principles and goals. Constructive criticism can be accepted and acted upon without internalising it as a verdict on personal worth. Malicious or ill-informed criticism can be acknowledged as an expression of another's state without being granted the power to destabilise one's inner ground. In both cases, the individual remains the ultimate arbiter of what to take on board.

In professional and academic contexts, this stance can foster a paradoxical form of social influence. People who are grounded in their own values and unshaken by minor disapproval often project a quiet authority that draws respect. Their presence communicates that while they value collaboration and mutual respect, they do not barter their self-respect for temporary approval. This balance—detachment from outcome, engagement with process—often makes their contributions more persuasive, not less.

Stoic detachment also challenges the performative mindset that dominates much of modern social interaction, especially in the age of social media. When every gesture, remark, or opinion is subject to immediate public reaction, the temptation is to curate an image designed to elicit maximum approval. This breeds anxiety and inauthenticity. By adopting the Stoic view, one's aim shifts from constant image management to consistent alignment with personal principles. Approval becomes a by-product of integrity rather than its primary goal.

Training this mindset is an ongoing process. It requires conscious practice in low-stakes situations before it can be relied upon in high-stakes ones. One might start by sharing a mild, genuine opinion in a conversation where agreement is expected, or by resisting the urge to over-explain when a comment is met with silence. Each of these moments reinforces the principle that another's reaction is information, not a verdict. Over time, the psychological distance between *what I do* and *what others think of it* grows, granting greater freedom in both speech and action.

The integration of Stoic detachment and empathy has another significant benefit: it prevents the defensive cynicism that sometimes develops in those who tire of seeking approval. A person who abandons care for others entirely may feel temporarily liberated but risks isolation and mistrust. By contrast, Stoic empathy preserves genuine human connection—valuing others' experiences without outsourcing one's identity to them. In this way, detachment becomes a source of steadiness, not alienation.

In sum, Stoic detachment in social contexts is neither aloofness nor resignation. It is an active stance rooted in self-governance: *I choose my words and actions in alignment with my principles, and I receive others' opinions as data rather than as destiny.* This approach not only dismantles the anxiety loop fuelled by constant self-evaluation but also enhances the quality of our interactions. We become freer to speak honestly, listen deeply, and act decisively—precisely because our worth no longer hangs in the balance of every raised eyebrow or faint smile. This is not the abandonment of social sensitivity; it is the reclaiming of social freedom.

Chapter 9
Resilience Through Ritual

When the mind is strained by uncertainty, decision fatigue, and the low-level hum of chronic stress, it does not usually cry out for more willpower—it longs for something to lean on. The popular narrative suggests that success in the face of adversity is powered by sheer mental grit, but anyone who has tried to "push through" anxiety with determination alone knows its limits. Willpower is volatile, easily eroded by poor sleep, low blood sugar, or an unexpected setback. Ritual, by contrast, is a structural anchor. It creates an environment where important actions happen automatically, without the constant negotiation and mental friction that make anxious minds stall. The very predictability that might seem mundane to some is, for those under mental strain, a source of profound relief.

In the Stoic tradition, resilience is not a passive state of enduring hardship; it is the cultivated ability to respond to life's disruptions with composure and clarity. The ancients understood that in moments of volatility, decision-making suffers. Epictetus advised setting a steady frame for one's days—clear opening and closing acts—that would hold regardless of the turbulence in between. Modern behavioural science confirms this wisdom: habits formed into rituals free cognitive bandwidth, reduce the opportunity for avoidance behaviours, and give the nervous system regular signals of safety. The anxious mind thrives not when each day is novel and unpredictable, but when it contains enough fixed points to prevent the sensation of being endlessly adrift.

The advantage of ritual is not merely practical; it is also psychological. Structured habits reduce the cognitive load in anxious moments by replacing deliberation with execution. Consider the contrast between starting the morning with a carefully pre-set mental preparation routine versus waking to a scatter of obligations, messages, and decisions. In the first scenario, the day's tone is claimed rather than dictated by circumstance. A well-designed morning ritual—whether a Stoic-style reflection, a deliberate breathwork practice, or a single page of purposeful writing—can serve as a psychological warm-up, aligning thought, emotion, and action before the demands of the world intrude. This is not about perfection or excessive self-optimisation; it is about protecting mental sovereignty in the day's most formative moments.

Ritual also addresses a problem that willpower cannot touch: the emotional turbulence caused by life's volatility. An anxious mind will often interpret unpredictability as threat, triggering heightened vigilance and draining energy reserves. Anchoring in predictability—through repeated, meaningful daily practices—provides a steady counterweight to external chaos. The predictability does not eliminate the chaos, but it gives the individual a stable base from which to meet it. This is why long-standing personal rituals—such as the same pre-meeting grounding exercise, a particular walking route during lunch, or a fixed end-of-day reflection—can be so potent. They tell the body and mind, *this is familiar, we are safe here,* and that signal of safety can dampen the hyper-reactive patterns that feed anxiety loops.

Just as the start of the day benefits from intentional framing, so too does its end. Many anxious people carry unresolved thoughts and tensions into the night, effectively working double shifts—one in the day's external demands, another in the mental churn of replayed conversations, unfinished lists, and speculative scenarios. An end-of-day ritual functions as a closing act, signalling to the nervous system that the active phase is over and that it is time to shift into recovery. This might take the form of a short reflective practice, a physical space reset, or a deliberate entry into a calming activity that marks the boundary between work and rest. Without such a boundary, the mind struggles to distinguish one day from the next, and rest becomes fragmented rather than restorative.

There is an elegance in how rituals scale across contexts. They can be deeply personal—crafted for the contours of one's own temperament and responsibilities—or collective, shared within households, teams, or communities to create shared stability. In both cases, they work not because they are rigid, but because they are reliable. The goal is not to cling to them in all circumstances but to maintain them in enough of life's turbulence that they become self-reinforcing. Each time you keep a ritual, you prove to yourself that stability is possible, even in disorder. Over time, this proof accumulates into a quiet, grounded confidence that no surge of anxiety can easily dismantle.

In this chapter, we move beyond the abstract encouragement to "have better habits" and into the precise architecture of rituals that cultivate resilience. We will examine why structured routines often outperform raw determination, how to construct a morning mental priming sequence that holds under stress, the ways in which predictable anchors can buffer against volatility, and the subtle but powerful effect of signalling closure to the mind before rest. Resilience, as you will see, is not forged only in dramatic tests of character. It is built, piece by piece, in the quiet repetition of actions that secure our footing before, during, and after the challenges we face.

Why Ritual Beats Willpower – Shows how structured habits reduce cognitive load in anxious moments

Willpower is often romanticised as the decisive ingredient of personal transformation, yet those who have tried to rely on it in the heat of anxiety quickly discover its fragility. It is a finite, depletable resource, vulnerable to fatigue, distraction, and stress. In moments when the nervous system is already overloaded, willpower is like trying to balance a tower of stones on a shaking table: even the smallest disturbance can topple it. Ritual, by contrast, bypasses this precarious balancing act. A ritualised behaviour requires minimal deliberation; it draws upon pre-encoded patterns rather than constant conscious effort, reducing the cognitive load exactly when mental clarity is most needed. This is why a structured, well-rehearsed habit can hold steady when determination alone falters.

Cognitive load theory offers a useful lens here. The brain can only manage a limited amount of information at any one time before performance declines. Anxiety already consumes a disproportionate share of that bandwidth, hijacking working memory with intrusive thoughts, imagined outcomes, and physiological discomfort. The anxious person must often navigate complex decisions while simultaneously managing a flood of internal stimuli—sweaty palms, racing thoughts, shallow breath—which leaves little mental space for considered action. Ritual intervenes by pre-solving certain decisions.

If the start of your workday is anchored in a specific sequence—open the journal, write three bullet points for focus, drink water, review schedule—the mind has fewer forks in the road to navigate. This frees cognitive capacity for the genuinely novel challenges ahead, rather than expending it on whether to open your email before breakfast.

The reliability of ritual is further amplified by its impact on the body's stress systems. Each repetition of a ritualised behaviour strengthens the neural pathways that support it, making it more automatic over time. The basal ganglia, the brain region heavily involved in habit formation, can trigger these behaviours with minimal input from the prefrontal cortex—the area responsible for conscious decision-making. This neurological delegation is crucial in moments of anxiety, when the prefrontal cortex is often compromised by the fight-or-flight response. A well-established ritual can still be executed even when the thinking brain is partially offline, functioning almost as a preloaded emergency programme that keeps behaviour aligned with values rather than panic.

Consider how elite athletes and performing artists use rituals before high-pressure events. Tennis players bounce the ball a precise number of times before serving. Musicians often rehearse the same warm-up sequence before stepping on stage. To an outsider, these acts may seem trivial or even superstitious, yet they serve a deeply practical purpose: they anchor the performer in familiarity, signalling to both brain and body that this is a known process. The repetition dampens uncertainty, helping maintain focus when the stakes are high. In the context of anxiety management, the same principle applies. Whether it is a breathing pattern before entering a meeting or a fixed sequence of steps before making a difficult phone call, ritual supplies the psychological scaffolding that willpower alone cannot reliably provide.

Philosophically, the Stoics intuited this centuries ago. They warned against the arrogance of believing that one could always summon the "right state of mind" on demand. Marcus Aurelius wrote daily not because he lacked insight, but because the act itself was a ritual that reinforced and stabilised his philosophical commitments. Without such reinforcement, he recognised that the mind's inclinations could drift under pressure. The discipline of repeating structured practices made virtue more dependable, in the same way that rehearsing a speech solidifies it far beyond first drafting. For the anxious mind, this reliability is invaluable: it transforms self-regulation from a matter of momentary choice into a matter of conditioned action.

Ritual also outperforms willpower in contexts where emotional avoidance threatens to derail action. Anxious individuals often hesitate to face discomfort, finding themselves in extended debates over whether they are "ready" to proceed. Willpower in these moments becomes an internal tug-of-war, with one part pushing for action and another resisting it. Ritual short-circuits this debate by embedding exposure to discomfort inside a larger, predictable framework. If your morning ritual includes ten minutes of deliberate conversation with colleagues before starting solitary work, the act becomes less about *mustering courage today* and more about *completing the sequence you always complete.* The discomfort is still present, but it is wrapped in the structure of the familiar, making it easier to tolerate.

The strength of ritual in anxious moments lies partly in how it aligns with how humans are wired to manage uncertainty. We evolved in environments where survival depended on repeating certain actions predictably—checking food sources, maintaining shelters, tracking the movement of the sun—because unpredictability increased risk. In the modern world, where uncertainty often takes the form of social evaluation, job insecurity, or shifting life circumstances, the nervous system still responds to unpredictability as if it were danger. Ritual restores a measure of predictability, signalling to the brain's threat-detection systems that the environment is stable, which in turn allows the body to downshift from a state of constant vigilance.

Importantly, the value of ritual is not in its rigidity but in its capacity to flex without collapsing. A ritual should be resilient enough to survive imperfect conditions. If your normal wind-down routine involves thirty minutes of reading in silence but you only have ten minutes one evening, the act of preserving *some* version of the ritual still sends the same stabilising signal. This adaptability ensures that the ritual remains sustainable over the long term—a key weakness of willpower-dependent strategies, which tend to fail entirely when conditions are less than ideal.

There is a modern temptation to conflate ritual with elaborate self-optimisation routines, but this misses the essence. A ritual is not valuable because it is lengthy or complicated; it is valuable because it is repeatable, reliable, and meaningful enough to matter under stress. Three slow breaths before answering a question in a tense conversation can be as powerful as an hour-long morning regimen, if the act is intentional and consistent. The point is to reduce cognitive friction when you are least able to afford it, not to burden yourself with additional complexity.

When examining why ritual so often outperforms willpower in anxious moments, the answer is both neurological and philosophical. Neurologically, rituals conserve mental resources and bypass impaired decision-making systems. Philosophically, they embody the Stoic idea that discipline is not the absence of struggle but the creation of structures that keep you aligned with your principles despite it. In the absence of such structures, anxiety will often dictate the course of action by default. With them, you create a counterweight—one that allows you to act from stability rather than reactivity, even when the mind is under siege.

Morning Mental Prep – Outlines a Stoic-style daily priming routine

The first minutes of the day are disproportionately powerful. Before the emails, before the headlines, before the demands of other people's agendas arrive, there exists a brief and unclaimed territory in which the mind can be set deliberately rather than reactively. Most people squander it. They scroll through notifications, let the day's first images and words be chosen for them, and then wonder why their thoughts are fractured by noon. The Stoics understood something modern neuroscience now confirms: the mental framing established in the morning acts as a cognitive and emotional template for the hours that follow. What you allow into the mind upon waking is not a neutral choice—it is the first lever of agency you either pull or surrender.

In a culture addicted to stimulation, a Stoic-style morning priming routine stands out precisely because it is unglamorous. It does not promise instant bliss, motivational highs, or a flood of dopamine;

instead, it trains the mind to expect challenge, choose perspective, and anchor in values before circumstance dictates mood. Marcus Aurelius opened his days with reminders of human fallibility and imperfection—not to breed cynicism, but to inoculate against frustration when reality inevitably presented flawed people and unforeseen obstacles. *If you rehearse the possibility of difficulty, difficulty itself loses much of its sting.*

From a psychological perspective, this is anticipatory regulation: the deliberate rehearsal of mental scripts before stressors occur. Studies in cognitive behavioural science have shown that expectation management directly influences emotional reactivity. A person who begins their day by visualising how they will respond to interruptions, criticism, or uncertainty is more likely to act in alignment with their intentions rather than in reflexive defence. The mechanism is simple but profound: priming shifts the nervous system from a reactive to a proactive state, allowing the prefrontal cortex—responsible for planning, empathy, and decision-making—to retain control even when the amygdala starts to raise alarms.

A well-constructed Stoic-style morning prep need not be lengthy. Its potency lies in consistency and structure, not in grandiosity. Five to ten minutes, repeated daily, will shape mental posture more reliably than sporadic hour-long bursts of good intention. The sequence might begin with stillness—a deliberate pause before engaging with external input. In practice, this could mean sitting upright, feet grounded, taking three slow breaths, and allowing the mind to settle without immediately grasping for distraction. This is not meditation in the popularised sense of chasing serenity; it is an assertion of sovereignty over attention before it is claimed by the world.

Next comes orientation: a conscious engagement with what matters today. For the Stoics, this often took the form of moral rehearsal—reflecting on virtues they wished to embody and the obstacles likely to test them. In contemporary terms, this could mean identifying the one or two qualities that will define your conduct regardless of outcome—patience in negotiations, clarity in decision-making, courage in delivering unwelcome truths. By naming these qualities at the start of the day, you transform them from abstract ideals into behavioural commitments. This is the bridge between philosophy and execution.

The third element is perspective. Here, the Stoics were unequivocal: you must remember the scale of your life in the wider order of things. This could be as direct as contemplating mortality—not in morbid fascination, but as a recalibration of priorities. Epictetus would remind himself that loss, discomfort, and even death are part of nature's law, and therefore not inherently catastrophic. Modern psychology would recognise this as a form of cognitive reappraisal—shifting the frame through which events are interpreted, thereby altering the emotional weight they carry. To integrate this into a morning ritual, one might briefly visualise a challenging scenario from the day ahead, then mentally walk through the most constructive response, reminding oneself that the choice of reaction remains within control.

Ritualising these steps is what separates a fleeting act of good intention from a reliable cognitive habit. Neuroscience shows that repetition under consistent cues—same time, same place, same initial actions—reinforces neural pathways until the behaviour becomes automatic. This is critical because the mornings you least "feel like" doing the prep are often the ones you need it most. A ritualised sequence requires less emotional negotiation and fewer cognitive resources to initiate, making it more likely to be upheld under stress.

It is worth addressing a common objection: that such preparation is artificial, even contrived. Shouldn't one simply live spontaneously and "face life as it comes"? The Stoics would argue that this is akin to entering a contest without training because "real life" will provide the challenge. Preparation is not the denial of spontaneity; it is the cultivation of readiness so that spontaneity does not collapse into chaos. Without deliberate priming, the mind defaults to its least disciplined patterns when tested—patterns shaped more by past conditioning than by present intention.

Practical application makes this clear. Imagine two professionals about to lead high-stakes meetings. One begins the day scanning news feeds, encountering half a dozen stressors before coffee, and steps into the meeting already primed for reactivity. The other spends five minutes recalling their core objective for the day, rehearsing a calm and clear response to anticipated pushback, and grounding attention before opening email. The latter has not eliminated anxiety, but they have created a mental map for navigating it. Over weeks and months, these small differences compound into a marked divergence in composure, decision-making, and resilience.

Morning mental prep also functions as a subtle act of boundary-setting. By choosing what enters your awareness first, you implicitly declare that your inner state is not at the mercy of external events. This is a critical assertion in an anxious mind, which often feels pulled in all directions by what "might" happen. The Stoic frame replaces that diffuse apprehension with a deliberate orientation towards what *will* happen—namely, the actions you will take and the character you will uphold.

In its purest form, Stoic-style priming is not about optimism or self-reassurance. It is about realism disciplined by agency. It accepts that the day will contain friction, that some variables will defy control, and that you may falter. Yet it commits, each morning, to the craft of responding well despite this. Over time, this discipline erodes the illusion that composure depends on perfect conditions. You learn, instead, that it is a function of repeated choice—and the morning is where that choice is most cleanly made.

Anchoring in Predictability – Uses stable rituals to counter life's volatility

Human beings tolerate uncertainty poorly, even those who pride themselves on adaptability. The brain evolved to seek patterns and anticipate outcomes because predictability was historically linked to survival; an unpredictable environment often meant danger. While modern life no longer threatens us with the same daily risks of starvation or predation, it confronts us with a subtler but equally taxing form of volatility—ever-changing workloads, fluctuating economies, unstable social dynamics, and the incessant churn of digital information. In such conditions, the nervous system can remain in a low-grade state of vigilance, scanning for the next unexpected demand. This is where stable rituals serve not as quaint routines or sentimental traditions, but as precision tools for regulating physiological and psychological stability.

A predictable ritual functions like a lighthouse in rough waters. It signals a fixed point amidst constant motion, allowing orientation even when everything else is in flux. Neurologically, rituals reduce the demand on the brain's decision-making circuits. The prefrontal cortex—responsible for complex reasoning and self-control—has limited daily capacity. Each unpredictable demand drains this resource, increasing susceptibility to impulsive reactions, cognitive fatigue, and anxiety spirals. By contrast, a fixed morning routine, an unchanging pre-meeting preparation, or a consistent end-of-day process strips away the need for micro-decisions in those areas, conserving cognitive bandwidth for higher-value tasks. *Predictability is not monotony; it is the deliberate removal of trivial uncertainty to preserve energy for meaningful engagement.*

Consider the counter-example: someone who begins each day deciding whether to exercise, what to eat, when to check email, and how to prioritise work, all while responding to external interruptions. Their mental energy is fragmented before any substantial progress is made. Compare this with the individual whose morning follows a practiced sequence—wake, hydrate, brief reflective writing, targeted reading, then work on the most demanding task before digital input. The latter enters the day not only with more focus but with a nervous system already acclimated to stability.

From a Stoic perspective, rituals serve as an embodiment of the principle of controlling what can be controlled. The Stoics acknowledged the volatility of external events, urging practitioners to focus on inner order. Anchoring in predictable actions is a way of asserting this order in tangible, repeatable form. Marcus Aurelius, despite leading a vast and unstable empire, clung to certain daily disciplines—writing his reflections at dawn, reviewing his conduct, and preparing himself for human imperfections he would encounter. These were not indulgent personal habits; they were stabilising anchors in an environment where chaos was guaranteed.

The power of predictability extends beyond cognition into physiological regulation. The autonomic nervous system—

constantly balancing between sympathetic (fight-or-flight) and parasympathetic (rest-and-digest) activation—responds strongly to consistent environmental cues. When the body experiences a repeated sequence at roughly the same time each day, it begins to anticipate the associated state. A nightly ritual of dimming lights, avoiding stimulating input, and engaging in a brief physical wind-down can train the body to prepare for sleep more efficiently, reducing insomnia linked to stress. Similarly, starting the workday with a fixed preparatory act—clearing the desk, reviewing three priorities, taking three deliberate breaths—signals to the body that it is time to focus, narrowing the mental aperture and reducing susceptibility to distraction.

One might object that over-reliance on ritual could breed inflexibility. Certainly, there is a danger in mistaking ritual for an unbreakable rule, especially if deviation induces unnecessary distress. However, the adaptive use of ritual is precisely the opposite: it creates a stable base from which flexibility is safer and less taxing. A mountaineer benefits from a solid anchor not because they remain fixed to it, but because it allows them to explore terrain without fear of being swept away. The most effective rituals are portable and modular—able to be shortened, adapted, or relocated without losing their stabilising essence.

Real-world application underscores this principle. A surgeon who performs the same pre-operative hand-washing sequence before every procedure is not indulging in superstition but entering a mental state of precision and readiness. A high-level athlete who repeats the same warm-up before each competition is not being rigid, but signalling to the mind and body that performance mode is engaged. In both cases, the ritual creates a controlled psychological environment before facing the uncontrollable.

The modern professional faces volatility not just from external events but from internal inconsistency. The pace of life encourages fragmented attention and reactive behaviour. A deliberately cultivated ritual—whether it is a midday recalibration pause, a Friday review of the week, or a set sequence before a challenging conversation—offers a form of internal predictability that counterbalances this. Such rituals become a form of self-leadership:

you decide how at least part of your day will unfold, regardless of the turbulence surrounding it.

Anchoring in predictability also has a social dimension. Group rituals, whether in teams, families, or communities, create a shared sense of stability. In workplaces, consistent opening and closing formats for meetings reduce uncertainty and promote engagement. In families, predictable mealtimes or weekly gatherings create relational anchors, especially valuable in times of collective stress. When external circumstances threaten to destabilise group cohesion, these shared rituals remind members of a dependable structure.

At its core, the use of stable rituals to counter life's volatility is not about clinging to comfort or avoiding change; it is about creating dependable rhythms that free the mind to face change with more composure. In an unpredictable world, those without anchors drift at the mercy of each wave. Those with well-placed, well-maintained anchors can turn their attention outward, navigating the shifting waters with both stability and skill.

End-of-Day Release – A simple practice to signal closure to the mind before rest

The human brain is not built to simply switch off when we stop working. In a culture where productivity often seeps into personal hours, the mental machinery remains engaged long after the last email is sent or the final task is completed. This is partly because unfinished thoughts generate what psychologists call the Zeigarnik effect—the mind's tendency to keep incomplete tasks active in working memory. Without an intentional closure ritual, this low-level cognitive tension can carry into the night, making relaxation elusive and sleep fragmented. *Ending the day is not just about stopping activity; it is about signalling to the nervous system that its role has shifted from vigilance to restoration.*

The absence of a clear "off-ramp" from the day's demands leaves the mind in a state of half-alertness. People often find themselves mentally re-running conversations, rehearsing tomorrow's tasks, or revisiting unresolved challenges in bed. The body may be horizontal, but the mind is still at its desk. This is more than a nuisance—it disrupts the body's circadian rhythm by delaying the shift into parasympathetic dominance, the state needed for deep rest and physiological repair. A structured end-of-day release is therefore not a luxury; it is a form of neural hygiene, as vital to long-term resilience as any morning routine or midday pause.

The most effective closure rituals operate on two levels: cognitive and physiological. Cognitively, they provide a container for the day's loose ends, giving the brain a sense of completion even if every task remains unfinished. This might involve reviewing what was achieved, capturing outstanding items for tomorrow, and articulating—aloud or in writing—what can now be left until the next day. By naming the transition, you create psychological permission to disengage. Physiologically, closure rituals employ sensory cues that shift the body's internal state—lowering light levels, altering posture, engaging in slower, deliberate movement. These physical changes act as signals to the hypothalamus and brainstem that the demands of alertness are over.

For some, this may take the form of a brief written "mind dump" followed by a fixed physical act, such as shutting a laptop and placing it in a drawer, or dimming the lights in the workspace. The repetition of the sequence matters: over time, the brain learns to associate these cues with the end of professional activity, much as Pavlov's dogs learned to associate a bell with food. Without such associations, work and rest blur into one long, indistinct continuum—a breeding ground for burnout.

Critically, end-of-day release is not simply the absence of stimulation. It is an active, intentional process of disengagement. Simply collapsing on the sofa with a device in hand does not allow the brain to recalibrate; in fact, the endless scroll of digital content may keep the nervous system on alert. A meaningful closure practice creates a clear symbolic and physiological boundary between "work mode" and "life mode." This can be as brief as three minutes, but it must be consistent enough to become a conditioned signal.

Real-world examples highlight its versatility. A senior barrister might end the day by organising case files for the next morning, closing the leather brief, and taking a deliberate slow walk to the station without checking messages. A designer working from home might switch off the desk lamp, water a plant, and change into different clothes before preparing dinner. These are not acts of avoidance; they are acts of containment. They give the brain a clear answer to the question, *Am I still on duty?*—and that answer, consistently, becomes *No.*

There is a Stoic dimension to this as well. Epictetus urged the examination of the day's actions before sleep, both as a moral inventory and a psychological clearing of the ledger. This was not an exercise in self-criticism but in closure—identifying what was within one's control, releasing what was not, and ensuring that no unresolved emotional residue carried into the night. Modern neuroscience supports the utility of such reflection; processing events before bed reduces the likelihood of intrusive thoughts later.

The beauty of end-of-day release lies in its adaptability. It can be scaled to the individual's environment, personality, and workload. For some, it might include gentle stretching or breathwork; for others, a short piece of music played every evening at the same time. What matters is the repeatability and the symbolic finality. A practice that changes daily lacks the conditioning power that makes these rituals effective. Consistency creates recognition, and recognition creates release.

Without such practices, the mind tends to operate on what might be called an "always-on residue"—a persistent background hum of unresolved intention. Over time, this undermines not only rest but also next-day performance. Deep rest is not the result of chance; it is the outcome of a deliberate disengagement process. To consistently perform under conditions of high demand, one must learn not just how to start the day with focus, but how to end it with closure. This is not indulgence—it is strategic recovery, the quiet act that sustains the capacity to meet tomorrow's volatility with a steady hand.

Chapter 10
The Courage Ledger

Progress in managing anxiety is too often measured by absence—fewer panic attacks, diminished tension, fewer avoided situations. On the surface, this seems like success. Yet defining achievement in terms of what does not happen risks a quiet but insidious trap: living within a slightly larger, marginally more comfortable version of the same constrained space. True progress is not "How calm was I this week?" but "Where did I act despite discomfort?" The Courage Ledger reframes the question, shifting attention from avoidance to action, from symptom suppression to engagement aligned with personal values.

Avoidance exacts a subtle but relentless toll. Each skipped opportunity, each declined invitation, each sidestepped challenge accrues costs—not abstractly, but concretely. Careers stagnate when presentations are evaded, relationships falter when vulnerability is withheld, skills plateau when difficult practice is avoided. Confronting these costs may be uncomfortable, but it is necessary. When avoidance is tied to tangible losses—time, income, relationships, missed growth—it becomes harder to rationalise staying in the comfort zone. People tolerate amorphous "anxiety," yet they are far less willing to accept the measurable price it exacts on their lives.

Where traditional tracking of anxiety charts symptom reduction, the Courage Ledger measures courageous acts themselves. This subtle shift in focus alters the psychology entirely: rather than waiting to feel better before acting, you act first and record that act as the metric of progress. Discomfort is reframed as a by-product of action, not a sign of failure. Behavioural science supports this approach: process-based metrics, under one's control, produce more sustainable change than outcome-based metrics, which are often swayed by external factors beyond one's influence.

The Ledger's potency lies in its discipline. A weekly review demands a level of honesty that sporadic reflection cannot achieve. At week's end, you examine where avoidance emerged, where it was resisted, and what patterns have formed. This is not a forum for self-recrimination; it is a space for pattern recognition—identifying triggers, decision points, and moments when hesitation gave way to action. Over time, this transforms vague self-awareness into actionable insight. Anxiety ceases to be an amorphous fog; it becomes a map, marked with identifiable pressure points and navigable detours.

There is also a philosophical shift embedded in this practice: discomfort is treated as data, not damage. Speaking up in a tense meeting, remaining present at a networking event despite unease—these are not incidental occurrences but entries in a ledger of courage. The week's most challenging moments become its most instructive, providing the raw material from which resilience is forged. Without these experiences, psychological growth lacks the necessary "overload" to strengthen the mind's capacity for action under stress.

The Courage Ledger does not seek a flawless record, nor does it aim to eliminate fear. Its purpose is to make fear visible, quantify its cost, and track the actions that counteract it, gradually raising the standard of what constitutes a well-lived week. After a year of consistent entries, the accumulated data tells a story far richer than symptom reduction alone—it documents a life lived deliberately, with increasing capacity to act despite uncertainty. The goal is not merely to feel courageous; it is to have proof that you have done so.

Measuring Avoidance Costs – Quantifies the life impact of avoidance to motivate change

Avoidance is often treated as a neutral act—an invisible decision that leaves no trace except the temporary relief it provides. Yet the real cost of avoidance is rarely neutral. It extracts a compound interest on opportunities missed, skills undeveloped, relationships weakened, and confidence eroded. What makes avoidance so insidious is its quiet nature; unlike an obvious failure, it leaves nothing tangible to confront. The job application never sent, the conversation never started, the project never pitched—these absences are not visible, yet they quietly shape the architecture of a life. The mind tends to discount what it cannot see, but when you begin to measure the cumulative effect of avoidance, the numbers are sobering. *The very situations you think you are sidestepping to protect yourself may be the ones whose absence costs you the most.*

To understand avoidance as an economic, emotional, and experiential drain, it helps to assign it a measurable value. This is not simply about calculating lost earnings, though that can be striking enough. Consider the professional who avoids applying for roles that require public speaking. Over a decade, they may miss promotions worth tens of thousands of pounds in salary increases. But beyond the money is a subtler toll: diminished influence, fewer professional connections, and a reduced sense of agency. The costs are cumulative and multidimensional. Avoidance strips away not only material opportunities but also the psychological resources that would make future challenges easier to meet. The more you avoid, the less prepared you are for what comes next—creating a self-reinforcing cycle in which future avoidance feels ever more necessary.

This quantification can be confronting. To put a number to avoidance forces you to acknowledge that each choice has a trajectory. If you avoid a networking event once, perhaps you miss a single connection. If you avoid it fifty times over five years, you may have quietly removed yourself from entire professional ecosystems. Similarly, someone who sidesteps difficult personal conversations may find, years later, that their relationships are functional but hollow, drained of the trust and authenticity that only emerge when discomfort is faced head-on. The Stoics reminded us that our time is our most precious asset; when avoidance consumes it, the loss is irretrievable.

There is a tendency to rationalise avoidance as a form of "waiting for the right moment." Yet when examined closely, this moment rarely arrives. The external circumstances might shift, but the internal conditions—uncertainty, discomfort, self-doubt—remain largely unchanged. In economic terms, the opportunity cost compounds with every delay. The writer who waits for confidence before submitting their manuscript forfeits years of feedback, improvement, and potential readership. The individual who avoids travel until "things settle down" forfeits memories and insights that can never be retroactively created. *Avoidance is rarely a pause; it is more often a quiet resignation disguised as a tactical delay.*

The measurable approach to avoidance reframes it from a vague emotional habit into a concrete behavioural pattern. Start by identifying areas of life where avoidance is most prevalent—career advancement, relationships, health, personal growth. Then estimate, even conservatively, the tangible and intangible losses associated with each. In career terms, this could involve lost earnings, missed skill acquisition, or decreased visibility. In relationships, it might mean reduced intimacy, unresolved conflicts, or diminished trust. In health, avoidance can manifest as postponed medical appointments, inconsistent exercise, or unaddressed mental health concerns—all of which have long-term costs far exceeding the discomfort of initial action.

For professionals and high-achievers, this exercise often reveals that the most costly avoidance is not in moments of obvious fear but in subtle hesitations. Declining to speak up in a meeting may seem inconsequential until you see that the cumulative effect is years of underrepresentation in decision-making spaces. Skipping small but valuable networking opportunities might seem like a reasonable conservation of energy until you calculate how many potential mentors, collaborators, or clients you have never met as a result. Once avoidance is logged in this way, its apparent safety becomes much harder to defend.

Yet there is an important nuance: not all avoidance is irrational or harmful. Strategic withdrawal—choosing not to engage in situations that are misaligned with your values or genuinely detrimental to your well-being—can be both wise and protective. The danger lies in avoidance driven by discomfort rather than discernment. The challenge is to differentiate between the two, and measurement is a powerful tool for making that distinction. When the costs of avoidance clearly outweigh the discomfort of engagement, the rational choice becomes visible, even if it remains emotionally difficult.

Behavioural science supports the idea that awareness of cost can shift decision-making. Studies in risk perception show that when people are made aware of the long-term consequences of inaction, they are more likely to choose short-term discomfort over sustained loss. This is partly because the human brain is wired to undervalue intangible or delayed rewards while overvaluing immediate relief. Quantifying avoidance counteracts this bias by making future losses feel immediate and concrete. In effect, you are pulling the long-term cost into the present moment, where it can influence your behaviour now rather than in hindsight.

The process of measuring avoidance costs is not about shaming yourself into action. It is about creating a realistic ledger of the life you are building through your decisions. Just as a business monitors both revenue and losses to stay financially healthy, individuals can monitor both gains from action and losses from avoidance to maintain psychological and practical health. In doing so, you reframe courage not as a lofty ideal but as a rational investment strategy: accept manageable short-term discomfort to secure long-term rewards.

This shift has a profound motivational effect. When you see avoidance not as a neutral choice but as an expensive habit, the cost of inaction begins to outweigh the fear of action. You become less willing to pay the price in opportunities, relationships, and experiences for the sake of fleeting comfort. This is where the Courage Ledger gains its teeth—not in recording grand acts of bravery, but in documenting the small, consistent acts that tip the balance away from avoidance and towards a richer, more engaged life. In the end, the numbers do not lie: a life measured only by what it has avoided is a life with less to show, and a life with less to remember. The goal is not to eradicate fear, but to make sure it is never the most expensive thing you own.

Tracking Wins, Not Just Symptoms – Shifts focus from anxiety reduction to courageous action taken

One of the most damaging habits in managing anxiety is measuring progress solely by the absence of discomfort. When the benchmark for success is "I felt less anxious today," the unspoken goal becomes to engineer life so that anxiety never shows up. The problem is that anxiety, being a normal human response to uncertainty, will always find ways to appear. This symptom-focused approach keeps attention locked on internal sensations—heart rate, stomach tension, intrusive thoughts—rather than on the external actions that move life forward. *The paradox is that by monitoring symptoms obsessively, you actually give them more significance and power, while neglecting to track the very behaviours that could make them matter less.*

Courage, unlike symptom reduction, is measurable in terms of action, not sensation. Did you make the difficult phone call? Did you speak up in the meeting? Did you attend the event you were tempted to skip? Each of these is a concrete, observable step that represents a win regardless of whether anxiety tags along. The Stoics would recognise this as shifting the locus of control from what you feel to what you do. Feelings are influenced by countless variables beyond your direct power; actions, however, remain yours to choose. This shift in measurement fundamentally changes your relationship with anxiety—it becomes background noise rather than the metric of your worth or progress.

Consider two people who both fear public speaking. The first aims to reduce anxiety and measures success by how calm they feel before a presentation. The second measures success by whether they delivered the presentation, regardless of their emotional state. In the short term, both might still experience anxiety. But over time, the second person is likely to build skill, confidence, and resilience, while the first may avoid opportunities altogether in pursuit of symptom-free experiences. *It is possible to live a meaningful, fulfilling life without ever reaching a state of zero anxiety, but impossible to do so while consistently avoiding meaningful challenges.*

Tracking wins is also a more accurate predictor of long-term improvement. Symptom fluctuations are notoriously unstable—affected by sleep, diet, weather, hormonal changes, even random chance. If you tie your sense of progress to these variables, your confidence will rise and fall without clear reason. In contrast, recording courageous actions creates a stable data set: a ledger of decisions made in the direction of your values. Over weeks and months, this ledger becomes proof that you can act despite discomfort, which is the real skill required for a resilient life.

This approach also reframes the role of anxiety. Instead of being the enemy to be eliminated, anxiety becomes a signal that you are stretching into unfamiliar territory. The absence of anxiety might simply mean you have stopped challenging yourself. Athletes understand this intuitively: muscle soreness after training is not a sign of failure but evidence of growth. In the same way, discomfort after taking a social or professional risk can be read as data that you are building capability in that area. When you track wins, you treat these moments as records of training, not as setbacks to be erased.

In practice, tracking wins requires specificity. "I did something scary" is too vague; "I initiated a conversation with a senior colleague instead of waiting to be spoken to" is actionable and measurable. The point is to create a narrative of agency, not a scrapbook of abstract aspirations. Some find it useful to keep a dedicated Courage Log—a daily or weekly record where they note the specific actions they took despite feeling hesitant or afraid. This not only reinforces the behaviour but also creates a powerful resource to revisit when self-doubt resurfaces.

There is a legitimate counterpoint to address: is focusing on wins simply another way of pressuring oneself into relentless productivity? The answer depends on what you define as a win. In this context, a win is not about volume of output or external achievement but alignment with your values in the presence of discomfort. For one person, a win might be asking a direct question in a group discussion. For another, it might be declining an invitation that would cause burnout. Both involve exercising choice in the face of anxiety, and both deserve recognition. The emphasis is on intentional action, not on meeting arbitrary quotas.

Psychologically, tracking wins also taps into reinforcement mechanisms that accelerate change. Behavioural science tells us that what gets measured gets repeated. When you make a habit of recording actions you are proud of—especially those taken under pressure—you strengthen the mental link between discomfort and positive outcomes. Over time, the brain begins to anticipate the satisfaction of recording a win, which can tip the scales in moments when avoidance feels tempting. This is not unlike athletes who train not just for the game but for the post-game analysis and recognition of performance gains.

This method stands in stark contrast to the common therapeutic trap of endless symptom monitoring. While self-awareness is important, it can easily become self-surveillance, where every spike in heart rate or flicker of worry is treated as a setback. By consciously shifting the frame to wins, you deprive symptoms of their role as the sole scorekeeper. Even on high-anxiety days, you can still "win" by taking a single step aligned with your values. That keeps momentum alive and prevents the demoralising all-or-nothing thinking that undermines recovery.

The Stoics knew that we cannot control the outcomes of our actions, but we can control whether we act according to our principles. Tracking wins honours this distinction. It is an operationalisation of their teaching: focus on what is within your power, and measure yourself by that. Modern psychology echoes the wisdom—exposure therapy, behavioural activation, and acceptance-based interventions all prioritise action in the presence of discomfort as the primary path to lasting change.

Over time, a consistent record of wins does more than just change how you see your anxiety—it changes how you see yourself. You move from the identity of someone "managing" anxiety to that of someone *living courageously despite* it. This is not a semantic shift; it is a psychological reorientation that affects every decision you make. Anxiety becomes one variable in the equation, not the final verdict on what you can and cannot do. And with each recorded win, you reinforce the truth that courage is not the absence of fear but the decision to act while it is present.

The Weekly Reckoning – End-of-week review to spot avoidance patterns and progress

Most people glide from one week into the next without ever pausing to examine what actually happened in the space between Monday and Sunday. The momentum of daily tasks, commitments, and distractions becomes a conveyor belt—efficient for keeping life moving but poor for revealing whether that motion is carrying you towards the life you want. In the context of anxiety and avoidance, this unchecked continuity is costly. Avoidance operates most effectively in the background, quietly shaping decisions, redirecting actions, and preventing exposure to the very situations that would foster growth. A *Weekly Reckoning* interrupts that autopilot, bringing to the surface the patterns that determine whether your weeks are compounding into progress or stagnation.

The value of such a review is not in obsessively cataloguing every interaction or measuring performance against an idealised standard. Rather, it is in developing the habit of deliberate retrospection—looking back over the week with curiosity, not self-condemnation, and asking: *Where did I lean into challenge, and where did I sidestep it?* This is a more precise question than the common "How did my week go?" because it explicitly orients the analysis toward courage and avoidance. By focusing on this binary—approach or avoid—you quickly see the micro-decisions that accumulate into very different futures.

Avoidance often presents itself as rational delay, harmless preference, or pragmatic choice. Declining an invitation because "the timing isn't right," putting off a call "until I feel more prepared," or delegating a task "because someone else could do it better" may each have legitimate justifications. But over the span of several weeks, the repetition of such decisions builds a pattern of withdrawal that can be invisible in the day-to-day. The Weekly Reckoning makes it visible. This visibility matters because *patterns, not isolated events, are the clearest predictors of trajectory.*

The exercise requires two complementary lenses: identifying avoidance patterns and recognising courageous actions. Without the second lens, the review becomes a demoralising inventory of failures; without the first, it risks becoming a feel-good highlight reel that ignores the mechanisms holding you back. The point is to capture both—the moments where you consciously chose to step into discomfort and the moments where you defaulted to safety. For example, perhaps you notice that you consistently volunteer ideas in one-on-one meetings but go silent in larger group discussions. That observation, repeated across several weeks, reveals a specific growth frontier you can target with intention.

It is important to emphasise that the Reckoning is not about "catching yourself out" in the moralistic sense. The aim is awareness, not punishment. Avoidance is not a character flaw; it is a default coping strategy wired into human psychology. Our nervous systems evolved to prioritise safety over exploration, and without conscious counterweight, this bias can quietly dictate behaviour. The Weekly Reckoning functions as that counterweight—it slows the pace enough for you to notice when the brain's safety-first impulse has been steering your choices more than your values have.

The practice also introduces an invaluable temporal rhythm to your self-assessment. Daily reflection has its merits, but it can be myopic; you risk getting caught in the noise of transient moods and isolated events. Quarterly or annual reviews, on the other hand, are too infrequent to catch small course corrections before they matter. Weekly sits in the sweet spot: long enough to see patterns, short enough to adapt before those patterns become entrenched. You begin to notice not just *what* you avoided or approached, but *when*—for example, perhaps anxiety spikes midweek after a demanding Tuesday, leading to more avoidance on Wednesday and Thursday. Such insights can inform preventative adjustments, rather than reactive regret.

This kind of review is most effective when it is specific and anchored in concrete actions. "I was more confident this week" is a vague impression; "I initiated three conversations with clients despite initial hesitation" is a verifiable data point. Similarly, "I avoided less" is unhelpfully abstract; "I postponed giving feedback to my colleague twice" is actionable. Over time, these records form a ledger—not unlike the training logs athletes keep—allowing you to chart progress, identify recurring obstacles, and develop strategies with evidence rather than intuition alone.

There is, of course, the temptation to turn this into a perfectionist audit, where any instance of avoidance is treated as a personal failure. That approach is counterproductive, reinforcing the same fear of imperfection that fuels avoidance in the first place. A more skilful stance is to treat avoidance instances as data points, not verdicts. The question is not *Why did I fail here?* but *What conditions led to this choice, and how can I shift them next time?* This framing preserves self-respect while still holding you accountable to your values.

Interestingly, the Weekly Reckoning can also illuminate positive patterns you may not have consciously credited yourself for. Many people underestimate their own courage because they focus disproportionately on moments of hesitation. Seeing a week's worth of intentional actions recorded in one place can recalibrate your self-perception. This recalibration matters: the more you identify as someone who regularly faces challenges, the more consistent your approach behaviour becomes, creating a virtuous cycle.

The practice's impact is magnified when it is kept simple and consistent. A sprawling, overly analytical review will be abandoned after a few weeks; a concise framework is sustainable. Some find it helpful to ask themselves three questions each Friday or Sunday evening: *What did I approach despite discomfort? Where did I default to avoidance? What patterns are emerging?* The goal is not exhaustive detail but cumulative insight. In time, you will likely find that the patterns identified in one week echo in the next—until you deliberately intervene.

From a philosophical perspective, the Weekly Reckoning embodies a principle shared by Stoicism and modern behavioural science: self-mastery begins with self-awareness, and self-awareness must be grounded in reality, not ideals. By reviewing your actions through the lens of courage versus avoidance, you ensure that the "reality" in question is not just how you *felt* about the week, but what you *did*. Feelings can be unreliable narrators; actions are more objective witnesses.

Over months, this simple ritual can become one of the most transformative tools in your psychological repertoire. It not only reveals the specific situations that challenge you, but also sharpens your understanding of how you respond to them. With that knowledge, you can set precise, meaningful challenges for the week ahead, rather than vague resolutions to "be braver" or "do better."

You begin to live in deliberate cycles of action, review, and refinement—cycles that, over time, make avoidance harder to sustain and courage easier to choose.

Would you like me to continue with the same level of depth for the next subchapter, *Celebrating Discomfort as Data*?

Celebrating Discomfort as Data – Reframes anxiety moments as training records, not failures

Most people treat anxiety as a red flag—evidence that something is wrong, that they are failing to cope, or that they lack the competence to handle a situation. This framing is both inaccurate and counterproductive. Anxiety, particularly in contexts where growth is possible, is not a sign of personal defect but of an active learning process. When understood correctly, moments of discomfort become data points—evidence of where you are training, where your limits are being tested, and where your system is actively adapting. In this sense, anxiety can be recast not as a verdict on your capacity but as a record of engagement. The challenge lies in replacing the reflexive aversion to discomfort with the discipline of observing it, logging it, and using it to inform deliberate practice.

This reframing is not merely motivational rhetoric; it rests on robust psychological principles. Exposure therapy, one of the most empirically supported treatments for anxiety, hinges on repeated, intentional contact with feared situations. The physiological discomfort during exposure—racing heart, shallow breathing, mental agitation—is not a sign the process is failing but that the nervous system is being stimulated in a way that creates the possibility for recalibration. If the goal is resilience, then these spikes in discomfort are the equivalent of a muscle's microtears during strength training: uncomfortable, but necessary precursors to increased capacity. Without recording these moments, you risk forgetting their value, interpreting them as setbacks rather than progress markers.

Consider the professional who avoids public speaking due to performance anxiety. In the old frame, a week in which they experienced three episodes of rapid heartbeat, sweating, and self-doubt during presentations might be labelled a "bad" week. In the reframed perspective, those are three logged training sessions—evidence that they entered the arena rather than sidestepped it. Each occurrence offers specific, reviewable data: the context, the intensity, the coping strategies attempted, and the recovery time. Over weeks and months, these entries reveal patterns of adaptation—perhaps the spikes in discomfort shorten, the recovery quickens, or the scope of challenges undertaken broadens.

The practice of documenting discomfort has an additional cognitive benefit: it interrupts the brain's negativity bias. Left unexamined, memory tends to exaggerate the severity and duration of anxiety episodes, making them seem more overwhelming than they were. Objective logging forces specificity—rating intensity on a scale, noting duration, describing the trigger. This precision creates a more balanced historical record, allowing you to see that while discomfort was real, it was finite, and often less catastrophic than anticipated. That shift in perception directly undermines avoidance, because the mind no longer treats discomfort as an unknowable and uncontrollable threat.

From a Stoic perspective, treating discomfort as data also aligns with the principle of objective judgement. The Stoics urged practitioners to distinguish between what is and what is interpreted. The racing heart is an observable fact; the conclusion that it means you are incompetent is an interpretation. By recording the fact without automatically accepting the interpretation, you create room for a more reasoned assessment. Over time, the act of logging becomes a form of cognitive distancing—a reminder that feelings are events to be observed, not unquestionable verdicts to be obeyed.

The key to making this practice transformative rather than perfunctory lies in the quality of the questions you ask yourself during recording. "Was I anxious?" is too blunt an instrument; it yields little insight. Better prompts include: *What specific action preceded the discomfort? What value or goal was I protecting or pursuing in that moment? How did I respond during the discomfort, and how did that align with my intentions?* These questions direct your attention not merely to the sensation but to its context and its relation to your chosen values.

They shift the narrative from "I felt anxious" to "I felt anxious while doing something that mattered to me."

It is important, however, to acknowledge the tension inherent in this reframing. For those with chronic anxiety or trauma histories, discomfort can sometimes be overwhelming, and celebrating it without nuance risks romanticising distress that exceeds adaptive thresholds. The discipline here is in differentiating between discomfort that signals constructive challenge and distress that signals harm. The former is worth logging and studying; the latter may require recalibrating the training load or introducing additional support. This is where the analogy to physical training holds: progressive overload builds capacity, but lifting weights far beyond current ability risks injury.

In organisational settings, this approach can be applied to leadership development, team training, and performance reviews. For example, a manager undergoing executive coaching might log moments of tension during difficult conversations, not as evidence of poor leadership but as markers of professional growth. Over time, these logs help identify where communication bottlenecks occur, where personal defensiveness spikes, and where resilience has measurably increased. The practice encourages leaders to see discomfort as an operational metric, just as they would track financial indicators or project timelines.

One of the subtler benefits of this reframing is its impact on identity. If you repeatedly treat discomfort as failure, you reinforce an identity of fragility; if you repeatedly treat it as data, you reinforce an identity of someone engaged in active, intentional development. Identity shapes behaviour—someone who sees themselves as "in training" is more likely to embrace future challenges as opportunities to gather more data, rather than threats to be avoided. The ledger of discomfort becomes, over time, a personal archive of evidence that you are capable of confronting and adapting to challenge.

For those concerned that such tracking might lead to over-analysis, the safeguard lies in brevity and structure. A discomfort log does not need to be a lengthy narrative; a few lines noting the situation, intensity, duration, and behavioural response are sufficient. The goal is to create a usable dataset, not a psychological autobiography. What matters is not the volume of words, but the consistency of observation over time.

Ultimately, celebrating discomfort as data requires a shift in both emotional stance and cognitive habit. Emotionally, it demands that you resist the instinct to recoil from the memory of discomfort. Cognitively, it demands that you replace vague recollections with specific, reviewable records. When both are in place, each anxiety episode ceases to be a standalone ordeal and becomes part of a larger trajectory—a series of entries in a training log that, viewed cumulatively, chart the expansion of your capacity. What once felt like a destabilising force becomes a measurable signal of engagement with life at the edges of your current ability. And it is precisely at those edges, logged and revisited, that meaningful growth occurs.

Chapter 11
When Anxiety Meets Crisis

There is a distinction between the slow simmer of everyday anxiety and the sudden, white-hot surge of fear that accompanies an acute crisis. A looming work deadline might quicken your pulse; a sudden medical emergency can constrict your breathing and narrow thought to a razor-focused tunnel. In such moments, theory alone offers little comfort—what counts is whether you can access the mental and physiological control necessary to act decisively. The difference between paralysis and decisive action often hinges not on innate fearlessness but on preparation: not the fantasy of predicting every disaster, but the cultivation of mental protocols that reliably activate under pressure. This chapter examines those protocols—how Stoic calm can endure contact with crisis.

Crisis, whether public or private, tends to follow familiar psychological patterns. Time compresses, information is incomplete, stakes feel immense, and consequences can be unforgiving. Under such strain, the nervous system flips into survival mode—an evolutionary mechanism capable of either sharpening performance or precipitating collapse. Those who navigate crises successfully rarely do so because they lack fear; rather, they have learned to convert it into focused action. Firefighters navigating a collapsing building, medics under fire, parents making split-second decisions for a child—they all demonstrate the same principle: anxiety is not eradicated in crisis, it is channelled. Learning to channel your own is at the core of crisis resilience.

The first section introduces the Acute Calm Protocol, a rapid-response framework for moments when clarity seems impossible. These are not elaborate exercises, but simple, three-step anchors to deploy when the body's alarm bells are ringing. The principle is practical: give the mind something concrete to do, rather than allowing it to spiral. The distinction between "I cannot think" and "I know my first three moves" is the difference between being swept away and stabilising enough to respond. Emergency professionals practise precisely this approach: brief, repeatable actions that create footholds in otherwise unstable conditions.

Next, the chapter examines maintaining agency amid chaos. High-stakes scenarios often induce passivity, making it feel as though one has no influence over outcomes. Yet case studies—from soldiers to pilots to humanitarian workers—show that agency is often less about controlling events than controlling your role within them. A medic in a war zone cannot alter the battlefield, but they can manage triage within their immediate field of influence. Focusing on what is within reach preserves operational effectiveness and prevents the cognitive collapse triggered by fixation on the uncontrollable.

The Stoics grasped this instinctively. Their writings stress that moral clarity becomes both compass and anchor when circumstances unravel. Hence, anchoring in core beliefs is not abstract philosophy but a practical survival tool. In moments where information is scarce and decisions urgent, values act as a filter for action. Even amid uncertainty, one can still act in alignment with principles. Crisis strips away the superficial and exposes the fundamental: who you are when deliberation is a luxury you cannot afford. This section explores how to identify and rehearse those principles in advance, so they can be deployed without hesitation.

Finally, the chapter addresses the aftermath—the physiological echo of crisis. Even when immediate danger subsides, the body often remains primed, sensing threats that no longer exist. If left unmanaged, this state can extend into chronic anxiety, turning a single event into a prolonged disruption. The goal is not merely to manage the body's post-crisis state but to close the loop, preventing lingering tension from embedding itself. Learning to exit crisis mode is as vital as operating within it; without it, one risks living perpetually on high alert for an event that has already passed.

Throughout, the chapter dispels the myth of immunity to fear. Fear is not the enemy—it is an inevitable companion. The task is to shape your relationship with it, transforming it from a destabilising force into a signal for disciplined action. By chapter's end, you will possess not only a framework for pivotal moments but also an understanding of the psychological mechanics that underpin it. This equips you to face crises not with brittle denial, hoping to avoid panic, but with the grounded presence of someone trained to meet it head-on.

Acute Calm Protocol – A three-step rapid response for panic or high-stakes moments

Panic does not arrive politely. It does not knock and wait for you to compose yourself before entering; it floods the system, hijacking breath, thought, and coordination in seconds. In high-stakes moments—whether delivering critical news to a boardroom, making a medical decision in the small hours, or facing an unexpected public confrontation—your ability to act hinges not on eradicating fear, but on stabilising yourself fast enough to think. While training, knowledge, and preparation all matter, the immediate need is a rapid bridge from overwhelm to agency. This is where a deliberate, pre-rehearsed *Acute Calm Protocol* becomes indispensable: a structured series of steps that can be initiated under pressure without deliberation, allowing you to reclaim cognitive bandwidth before the crisis dictates your behaviour.

The physiological mechanics of panic are predictable. Heart rate spikes, blood flow shifts from the brain's higher reasoning centres towards muscles primed for action, and the body's stress hormones surge. This cascade, an evolutionary asset in moments of physical danger, is less helpful when the crisis demands nuanced decision-making rather than sprinting or fighting. The first function of a rapid-response protocol, therefore, is to interrupt the body's automatic escalation. Without this, even the most skilled professional can find their capacity for clear thought degraded to the point where memory, reasoning, and speech falter. Military instructors know this well; their trainees are drilled in short, repeatable grounding actions that anchor attention before giving orders. It is not courage alone that keeps a soldier effective in chaos—it is the muscle memory of self-regulation.

The first step of any effective acute calm sequence is a targeted physical intervention. General advice to "take a deep breath" is too vague to be useful when your lungs feel locked and your chest constricted. A more precise, actionable option is to exhale fully before inhaling slowly for a controlled count, ideally extending the exhale slightly longer than the inhale. This triggers the parasympathetic nervous system, signalling safety to the body. By forcing a longer exhalation, you tip the autonomic balance away from fight-or-flight and towards a state in which rational thought can return. This is the equivalent of hitting the reset button on a jammed system: it does not solve the problem, but it makes the interface usable again.

Once the body is partially stabilised, the second step is cognitive narrowing—not in the sense of tunnel vision, but of stripping away everything non-essential in your mental field. In crisis, the untrained mind attempts to process every possible variable at once, amplifying overload. A rapid cognitive narrowing technique might be as simple as identifying *the single next action* you can take within the next thirty seconds that moves the situation forward. The point is not to solve the entire crisis but to create momentum in a controlled direction. For a doctor in an emergency ward, that might mean calling for a specific piece of equipment; for someone facing a public speaking panic, it might be focusing on delivering just the first sentence, not the entire speech. This targeted micro-focus buys time and prevents cognitive fragmentation, which is often the true source of errors under pressure.

The third step is micro-commitment to action—deliberately engaging with the crisis in a way that confirms you are no longer in a purely reactive stance. Action here is not impulsive flailing; it is the smallest meaningful gesture that re-establishes your role as an active participant rather than a passive subject of events. Psychological research on agency shows that even minimal, purposeful action changes the brain's interpretation of a situation, shifting it from threat to challenge. The Stoics would recognise this as the transition from being "acted upon" to "acting." A pilot in turbulence might run through a pre-set checklist not only to manage the aircraft but to assert, mentally, *I am directing events within my sphere of control.*

These three stages—physiological reset, cognitive narrowing, and micro-commitment—form a loop you can run through multiple times if needed. They are not meant to eliminate fear entirely; they are meant to restore the bandwidth to make decisions aligned with your priorities, values, and training. Crucially, the protocol must be rehearsed when you are calm. In the absence of repetition, even the most elegant sequence will vanish under stress. Crisis responders practise their grounding steps in routine drills not because they expect to feel brave, but because they know courage is often just familiarity under pressure.

One of the underappreciated strengths of such a protocol is its universality. While the specific actions can be tailored to context, the sequence works across domains because it addresses the human stress response at its roots. Athletes on the starting line, negotiators in high-stakes talks, parents in emergency rooms—all experience the same physiological and cognitive constriction when under threat. By learning a rapid sequence that shifts both body and mind back towards operational capacity, you create a transferable skill that applies whether the "threat" is physical, professional, or interpersonal.

Some might object that in certain crises, action must be instant and instinctual, leaving no time for deliberate steps. But this misunderstands the nature of the protocol: it is designed to be instinctual through prior rehearsal, as reflexive as reaching for a seatbelt. The difference is that instead of being at the mercy of your most primal reactions, you are shaping those reactions to include a sliver of conscious choice. That sliver can determine whether your first move in a crisis makes the situation better or worse.

Importantly, the value of an Acute Calm Protocol extends beyond the moment of crisis. It creates a form of self-trust that accumulates over time. Each time you successfully run the sequence, you reinforce the belief that you can navigate high-pressure moments without losing your footing. This belief acts as a psychological inoculation, reducing anticipatory anxiety about future crises. You may not be able to guarantee the outcomes of emergencies, but you can reduce the fear of your own response, which in itself is a major source of anxiety.

The protocol also has the advantage of countering a cultural misconception about composure: that calm is the absence of physiological arousal. In reality, calm under pressure is the ability to function effectively despite arousal. Heart pounding, hands shaking, voice tight—none of these preclude decisive action if your mind is structured enough to operate through them. This reframing is liberating for those who assume they must "feel calm" before they can act. The protocol demonstrates that action can lead, and emotional stability can follow, rather than the other way around.

By embedding a rehearsed, three-step process into your crisis repertoire, you transform calm from a hopeful aspiration into a concrete skill. In doing so, you are no longer reliant on luck, natural temperament, or wishful thinking when pressure spikes. You have something to deploy—fast, deliberate, and repeatable—when panic comes uninvited, as it inevitably will. The result is not immunity from fear, but a sharpened ability to meet it on your terms.

Maintaining Agency in Chaos – Examples from crisis workers and soldiers applying Stoic calm

The difference between being swept along by events and steering through them often comes down to whether you can maintain a sense of agency in the most disorienting circumstances. When chaos erupts—gunfire in an urban patrol, a patient's condition plummeting in an emergency ward, a sudden loss of communication during a rescue mission—those who function effectively are not necessarily the most fearless. They are the ones who have trained themselves to preserve the ability to choose, to think, and to act in alignment with their purpose despite the storm raging around them. This is the core of what the Stoics meant when they urged *holding fast to what is within one's control.* In the language of modern performance psychology, it is about protecting your decision-making capacity when the environment is actively trying to strip it away.

Consider the account of a London Fire Brigade officer leading a team into a smoke-filled tower block during the Grenfell Tower fire. The structure was unstable, the air toxic, and visibility near zero. In such a setting, panic could cascade quickly through both mind and body, clouding judgment at precisely the moment when it must be most exact. Yet the officer described an internal narrowing: breaking the mission into immediate objectives—locate residents, guide them to an exit, return for the next group—while filtering out unmanageable factors like the scale of the blaze or the building's fate. This mental triage mirrored Stoic thinking: the conflagration was beyond his command, but the decision to take the next clear action was entirely his. By doing so, he not only increased the odds of survival for those inside but prevented the paralysis that often accompanies a mind overwhelmed by the whole picture.

Military examples are equally instructive, not because soldiers are immune to fear, but because their training acknowledges its inevitability. In 2009, during an ambush in Afghanistan's Korengal Valley, a platoon sergeant faced incoming fire from multiple elevations. Communications with command were patchy, and the unit risked being cut off. Rather than succumbing to the pull of reactive thinking—shooting blindly or running for cover without coordination—he focused on establishing a fire-and-move rhythm, directing each small element to reposition in turn. This kept the group cohesive and allowed them to withdraw to defensible ground. The sergeant later noted that his attention was anchored on the *order* of moves, not the noise of battle. In essence, he applied the Stoic discipline of attention: anchoring thought to the controllable sequence, not the uncontrollable variables.

Healthcare workers in crisis zones often demonstrate the same principle under different sensory and moral pressures. In Médecins Sans Frontières field hospitals, medics sometimes face an unending stream of casualties with limited supplies and no guarantee of evacuation. One nurse described her method for maintaining agency: she kept a short written list—triage categories and available resources—clipped to her pocket. In the middle of chaos, this list became a tether, a way to externalise critical decisions and avoid being drawn into despair at the scale of suffering. This practice illustrates an important distinction: agency does not always mean having multiple good options; sometimes it means keeping enough clarity to choose the least harmful path available.

The Stoic calm shown in these examples is not the absence of strong emotion. In fact, crisis workers and soldiers often report acute fear, sadness, or anger in the moment. The distinction lies in how they relate to those emotions. Rather than seeing them as directives to act upon, they treat them as environmental data—signals to be acknowledged but not obeyed blindly. This subtle shift—*I feel fear, but I choose my next move based on the mission*—is the practical application of Epictetus' reminder that events themselves are neutral; it is our judgments that give them power.

Maintaining agency also involves resisting the cognitive narrowing that chaos tries to impose. In moments of extreme stress, the brain tends to fixate on the most immediate threat, neglecting longer-term or broader situational awareness. Trained operators counter this by deliberately scanning for context cues: checking the flank during a forward push, reassessing the patient's vital signs even while addressing bleeding, noting exits while addressing the immediate hazard. These small acts of deliberate observation expand the decision-making space, preventing the mental claustrophobia that can lead to poor choices.

It is tempting to imagine that this kind of composure is innate, the preserve of a certain temperament. Yet the testimonies of experienced crisis professionals consistently point to the role of rehearsal, ritual, and shared frameworks. Firefighters walk through the same buildings repeatedly so that in zero-visibility conditions they can navigate by touch. Soldiers run drills not only for tactics but for communication under duress, ensuring that the words they use are short, unambiguous, and executable. Medical teams rehearse mass casualty scenarios so that when resources are scarce, the ethical framework for allocation is already agreed upon. These preparations do not eliminate the chaos; they inoculate the team against losing agency within it.

Even in situations where external control is almost entirely stripped away—hostage scenarios, disaster entrapments, or active shooter events—those who survive often report finding small anchors of agency. A soldier held in captivity for months described deciding each day to clean his cell corner, purely to remind himself there were still actions he could initiate. This micro-agency kept his identity intact, preventing the total collapse of will that indefinite uncertainty can produce. The Stoics would recognise this as holding to *prohairesis*—the faculty of choice—when all else is removed.

For those outside the worlds of warfare or frontline emergency work, these lessons are far from abstract. Corporate crises, family emergencies, or sudden public confrontations all have the same core features: incomplete information, high stakes, and emotional volatility. The same principles apply—focus on the controllable, rehearse responses before you need them, anchor in purpose rather than emotion, and deliberately widen your field of perception when pressure tries to narrow it.

By studying the patterns of those who have acted with clear agency in extreme conditions, we see that Stoic calm is not an inherited trait but a cultivated discipline. It is built in the quiet hours of preparation, tested in the crucible of real events, and maintained not by suppressing emotion but by subordinating it to a chosen direction. In this way, agency is not merely preserved in chaos—it becomes the lever by which chaos is shaped into something survivable, and sometimes, even into something transformative.

Anchoring in Core Beliefs – How moral clarity can outlast uncertainty in emergencies

In the split-second between recognising a crisis and acting within it, most of us rely not on detailed plans but on the deep, often unspoken convictions that shape our judgement. Training and skill matter, but when events unfold faster than conscious deliberation can keep pace, it is our core beliefs—those principles we regard as non-negotiable—that provide the compass. These beliefs can cut through confusion, neutralise hesitation, and preserve dignity even when the external situation is chaotic or morally ambiguous. In emergencies, when uncertainty is the prevailing condition, *moral clarity is not a luxury; it is a survival tool.*

The historical record is full of moments in which individuals, facing the collapse of normal order, acted decisively because they knew what they would and would not do—long before the crisis ever presented itself. During the 2011 earthquake and tsunami in Japan, the Fukushima Daiichi nuclear disaster placed technicians in an almost impossible position: stay and risk lethal radiation exposure, or evacuate and abandon critical containment work. Several older workers volunteered to remain, reasoning that they had fewer years of life expectancy than their younger colleagues. They were not fearless; they were anchored. Their decision was not made in the emotional churn of the moment but arose from a deeply held belief about duty, sacrifice, and generational responsibility. In this way, core beliefs functioned as a prewritten decision script, sparing them from paralysis and remorse.

Modern Stoicism recognises that without such internal anchoring, we are prone to be tossed between competing fears—the fear of immediate harm and the fear of acting wrongly. Anchoring in core beliefs compresses that moral calculus into something executable under pressure. A paramedic who has internalised that *the patient comes first* will prioritise treatment even when it means bending rules of protocol, because the belief has been rehearsed until it sits above situational noise. In contrast, the responder who has never clarified their hierarchy of values may spend precious seconds weighing outcomes, vulnerable to indecision and the influence of bystanders.

The danger of being unanchored in a crisis is not only indecision but drift—gradually adopting the values of the loudest voice or the most forceful presence in the room. In emergencies, social contagion can be as lethal as physical hazards. Crowd behaviour during the 2010 Love Parade disaster in Duisburg, Germany, where a stampede killed 21 people, was amplified by the fact that few individuals acted from a clear personal rule set; most followed the movements and mood of those around them. When pressure mounts and time compresses, the absence of core beliefs leaves a vacuum that the surrounding chaos readily fills.

Anchoring is not the same as stubbornness. A rigid commitment to an impractical plan can be disastrous, but a commitment to underlying principles can allow rapid adaptation without losing the thread of moral identity. Soldiers operating under the laws of armed conflict know they must distinguish combatants from civilians, but within that boundary they are trained to adjust tactics fluidly to the conditions. Here, the principle acts as a fixed point around which strategy can pivot. The ability to flex without breaking one's ethical frame is the difference between principled adaptability and mere expedience.

Establishing such an anchor before a crisis involves deliberate reflection, not on specific scenarios, but on the values one refuses to compromise. Many emergency workers use decision pre-sets: statements such as "I will not abandon someone in my care unless doing so preserves more lives overall" or "I will never falsify a record, regardless of pressure." These are not abstract ideals; they are operational lines in the sand. In practice, they reduce cognitive load in moments when adrenaline narrows attention and the brain's executive functions are under siege.

The durability of core beliefs in uncertainty also depends on how deeply they are integrated into one's self-concept. Beliefs that are externally adopted—because an organisation requires them or because they are socially rewarded—are more likely to crumble under extreme stress. Those that have been tested in smaller trials of adversity, however, become part of one's moral reflexes. This is why veteran crisis responders often display a steadiness that rookies lack: they have not only identified their beliefs but have stress-tested them in live conditions. Each experience reinforces the sense that *I know what I stand for, even here.*

From a Stoic perspective, anchoring in core beliefs aligns with the discipline of assent: the practice of granting mental agreement only to judgements that withstand rational scrutiny. In a high-pressure environment, this means refusing to let panic, peer pressure, or wishful thinking override what you already know to be right. The Roman statesman Cato the Younger exemplified this when he opposed Julius Caesar's rise to dictatorship, fully aware that his stance could—and ultimately did—cost him his life. Cato's actions were not improvised acts of defiance; they were the natural extension of a lifelong commitment to the republic's constitutional principles.

In modern crises, the same mechanism applies. A humanitarian aid coordinator in a conflict zone may face armed groups demanding the diversion of medical supplies. The immediate threat is palpable, but the long-term harm of compromising neutrality can be equally severe, eroding trust with all parties and endangering future missions. Coordinators who hold fast to the principle of impartial aid delivery find ways to de-escalate without surrendering their core commitment, even if it means walking away from a short-term gain.

The process of anchoring is not solely about self-protection; it can also create stability for others. In chaotic environments, people instinctively look for behavioural reference points. A leader who demonstrates moral clarity—by consistently acting in line with stated values—becomes a fixed marker in the storm, enabling team members to orient their own actions. This is particularly evident in disaster relief efforts, where consistent adherence to ethical guidelines in triage, distribution, and reporting fosters collective discipline and trust.

Moral clarity also mitigates the corrosive aftershocks of crisis work. Many responders suffer from moral injury—a deep psychological distress caused by acting against one's ethical code under duress. Having a pre-established anchor can reduce the likelihood of such injury, because decisions made in alignment with core beliefs, even under tragic constraints, are easier to reconcile in hindsight. This is not about avoiding guilt altogether—crisis work often involves unavoidable losses—but about ensuring that regret is not compounded by the knowledge that one abandoned one's principles when they were most needed.

Ultimately, anchoring in core beliefs transforms uncertainty from a disorienting void into a navigable space. The external situation may remain unstable, but the internal reference frame holds. In the absence of such anchoring, uncertainty breeds reaction; with it, uncertainty becomes a field in which deliberate action is still possible. The Stoics understood that while fortune may dictate circumstances, it cannot dictate the quality of our choices—unless we permit it to. And in the theatre of emergencies, where events evolve too quickly for comfort, the clarity of what you stand for may be the only stable ground you have.

Aftershock Recovery – Managing the body's post-crisis state to prevent lingering anxiety

The crisis may have ended, but the body often does not get the memo. Hours or even days after the last urgent decision is made, after the threat has passed and the environment appears calm, the nervous system can remain locked in a state of heightened vigilance. This aftershock is not mere "stress residue"; it is a physiological echo of survival mode, and if left unchecked, it can hardwire anxiety into a person's baseline state. Those who have lived through genuine emergencies—first responders, soldiers, medical personnel, or civilians caught in sudden disaster—often speak of a paradox: the event itself is easier to manage than the aftermath. In the moment of crisis, adrenaline sharpens focus and constrains the field of attention to what is immediately actionable. Once the danger passes, that chemical clarity recedes, leaving the body's stress machinery still humming, directionless and unspent.

This post-crisis physiology is not a flaw but a survival adaptation. The human stress response evolved to keep us alive in unpredictable environments, and its mechanisms are slow to stand down precisely because danger in the wild rarely ended with a clean cut-off. Our ancestors could not afford to assume a predator had truly gone after the first escape; maintaining a period of hyper-alertness improved survival odds. In modern crises, however, this delay in deactivation becomes a liability. Without deliberate intervention, the heightened state can turn into a persistent pattern—hypervigilance that bleeds into everyday life, fragmented sleep, irritability, and difficulty concentrating. The body begins to operate as if a new crisis is always imminent, and the mind follows suit.

What makes aftershock recovery particularly challenging is that it demands a shift from emergency mobilisation to restoration, a shift that does not occur automatically for many people. Professional crisis workers are trained to act under pressure, but fewer are trained in how to stand down afterwards without leaving unresolved stress lodged in the body. Military debriefing protocols, for example, often emphasise operational review and lessons learned, but they do not always address the neurophysiological residue of the experience. In some cases, the cultural expectation to "be fine" becomes its own form of suppression, pushing unprocessed arousal underground, where it emerges later as chronic anxiety or even post-traumatic stress.

Recovery, in this context, is not simply about rest; it is about recalibration. The nervous system needs an explicit signal that the threat window has closed. Stoic philosophy provides a mental anchor here: the principle of returning one's attention to what is within control. But the body must be persuaded as well, and it speaks in the language of sensation, not abstraction. Slowing the breath to a steady rhythm, grounding in physical contact with stable surfaces, or deliberately engaging in slow, repetitive movements can signal safety to the brainstem. This is not "relaxation" in the spa sense; it is an operational reset, instructing the system that it can release its grip on fight-or-flight readiness.

The military has long recognised that the state immediately following intense action is a critical juncture. Units returning from deployment are often kept together in controlled environments before being released into civilian life, precisely to allow for this decompression window. The absence of such transition is one reason why some first responders, especially in under-resourced regions, develop cumulative anxiety symptoms—they are sent from one high-stakes event to another without structured opportunities to metabolise the stress. In high-tempo roles, aftershock recovery may need to be deliberately carved out between missions, even if the schedule resists it.

There is also a cognitive dimension to aftershock recovery. The mind, freed from the immediate demands of crisis management, often replays events, searching for what could have been done differently. This review process can be adaptive if it leads to constructive learning, but without boundaries, it becomes rumination—a loop that reinforces the body's tension. Setting a deliberate container for review, such as a fixed 30-minute debrief with oneself or a trusted colleague, allows lessons to be drawn without inviting indefinite rehashing. Once that window closes, the attention must be redirected to present-moment activities that do not require hyper-alert scanning for danger.

An often-overlooked factor is the role of identity. People whose self-worth is bound tightly to their crisis competence may find it difficult to disengage because calm feels like purposelessness. Firefighters, for instance, sometimes describe feeling more at ease in the heat of an incident than in the quiet of the station. This can lead to self-induced stimulation—seeking new emergencies or amplifying minor stresses—to maintain the familiar arousal state. Recognising this tendency and consciously valuing recovery as part of professional skill, rather than an indulgence, is essential for long-term mental health and operational readiness.

Physiologically, the aftershock phase is marked by a cocktail of residual hormones—adrenaline, cortisol, and others—that do not vanish immediately. Active recovery techniques can help accelerate their clearance. Controlled physical exertion, such as brisk walking or light resistance training, uses up the leftover energy without perpetuating the stress loop. Cold-water immersion, increasingly studied in both athletic and trauma contexts, can induce a parasympathetic rebound, shifting the body into rest-and-digest mode more quickly. The key is intentionality: passive waiting for the body to "settle on its own" often prolongs the state, whereas targeted intervention shortens it.

From a Stoic stance, aftershock recovery is an exercise in reclaiming agency over one's internal state when the external drama has ended. Marcus Aurelius wrote about the need to return the mind to its governing principle after being disturbed. In modern terms, this means consciously deciding that the crisis no longer owns your body's chemistry. One practical method is the use of physical "ritual closures"—symbolic but embodied acts that mark the end of an event, such as changing out of work gear, washing the face, or deliberately altering posture and breathing before leaving the scene. These gestures, repeated consistently, condition the body to recognise that it is safe to stand down.

Neglecting aftershock recovery carries risks beyond personal wellbeing. In team settings, unprocessed post-crisis states can degrade communication, increase irritability, and impair decision-making on the next deployment. Leaders who model recovery behaviours—taking the time to recalibrate rather than rushing immediately into the next task—send a message that preservation of operational capacity is a shared priority. This culture of sanctioned recovery not only reduces burnout but also increases the quality of performance when the next genuine crisis arrives.

Ultimately, the ability to manage the body's post-crisis state is a strategic skill, not an optional luxury. The event may be over, but the nervous system's echo can shape behaviour for weeks, even years, if ignored. By treating aftershock recovery as an integral part of crisis competence—one that blends physiological reset with cognitive closure—we prevent temporary survival adaptations from calcifying into chronic anxiety. The crisis may have dictated the tempo during its peak, but in the aftermath, it is within our control to slow it, steady it, and step back into the rest of life on our own terms.

Chapter 12
The Stoic Loop Breaker

There is a fleeting instant in every anxiety loop when clarity remains—a narrow, fragile window in which a deliberate choice can prevent the mind from tumbling into full spiral. Too often, that moment slips away, devoured by the inertia of overthinking and the body's automatic stress responses. The Stoic Loop Breaker is designed to seize that instant, to place a hand on the mental brake before anxiety accelerates beyond control. This is no vague injunction to "stay calm" or "think positively"; it is a precise, actionable protocol, grounded both in ancient philosophy and contemporary behavioural science, built to function when the stakes are highest and pressure is intense.

The four steps—Label, Locate, Limit, Lean In—compose a disciplined sequence that replaces scattered instinct with deliberate control. Each step is straightforward, yet together they provide a portable mental toolkit, deployable anywhere: in the heat of a negotiation, on the brink of public speaking, or in the quiet panic of an overactive mind at 2 a.m. What sets this method apart is not merely its efficacy in acute moments but its adaptability. The Loop Breaker is not brittle; it scales. For mild anticipatory tension, the process can be applied lightly and almost imperceptibly. In high-stakes or full-blown panic scenarios, it expands into a deliberate, embodied intervention, restoring enough agency to select the next action rather than being swept along by reflex. This versatility ensures the method is relevant across contexts—from a university student facing an exam to a surgeon mid-operation, or a firefighter entering a volatile situation.

Label, the first step, draws from the Stoic practice of naming impressions before accepting them. Assigning a name to an anxious thought or bodily sensation interrupts the unspoken contract we make with fear when we treat it as reality. A racing heart becomes, "my heart rate is elevated," rather than, "I am in danger." Locate, the second step, anchors the experience in time and space, tethering awareness to the present rather than the catastrophes projected by the mind. Limit establishes temporal or behavioural boundaries—

deciding, for instance, to revisit a worry only after a specific event or confining rumination to a written page. Finally, Lean In challenges avoidance by engaging deliberately with the feared thought or action, dissolving its grip through controlled exposure rather than retreat.

What makes the Loop Breaker distinctive is that mastery of each individual step is not a prerequisite for effectiveness. The method integrates earlier practices—ritual, reframing, embodied grounding, and courageous action tracking—into a cohesive operational flow. Calm, in this sense, is not a static state but a series of repeatable behaviours executed with precision. Applied in real time, the steps become almost instinctive, yet the learning curve is accelerated through deliberate practice. This chapter presents both a detailed breakdown of the mechanics and case-study walkthroughs from diverse contexts—emergency medicine, high-pressure corporate decisions, everyday interpersonal conflicts—illustrating application in the real world. These accounts are procedural, honest, and unpolished, showing moments where execution was imperfect yet still sufficient to prevent escalation.

The true value of the Loop Breaker extends beyond interrupting single anxiety cycles; it reshapes one's relationship with anxiety itself. Practised across scenarios, it transforms spikes of fear from unpredictable assaults into structured events with known exit routes. Over time, anxiety ceases to dictate behaviour and becomes a signal, a prompt to engage a familiar process. The goal is not to eliminate fear but to neutralise its capacity to ambush. In the sections ahead, we will distil the method to its essentials, demonstrate adaptation from minor daily stressors to acute crises, and provide real-world examples of application. By the end, the Stoic Loop Breaker will not merely be a concept to understand—it will be a reflex you can trust.

The Four Steps: Label, Locate, Limit, Lean In

Anxiety loops are rarely broken by accident. They persist because they are self-reinforcing, a closed circuit where thoughts, sensations, and behaviours each amplify the other. The body interprets a rising heart rate as evidence of danger, the mind searches for a cause, and the search itself becomes the threat. Breaking that loop requires an intervention precise enough to disrupt the cycle without relying on vague affirmations or sheer willpower. The four-step process—Label, Locate, Limit, Lean In—is designed to provide that precision. It draws on the Stoic principle of *interposing reason between impression and assent*, while integrating insights from cognitive behavioural techniques, attentional control, and exposure-based learning. These steps do not ask you to deny anxiety, distract yourself from it, or wait for it to pass. They ask you to handle it directly, to convert a reflexive reaction into a deliberate response.

The first step, Label, operates on a deceptively simple premise: to name what is happening in plain, factual terms. This is not an exercise in creative expression or a search for deep causes—it is a surgical act of definition. When Marcus Aurelius advised himself to "call things by their true names," he was not engaged in poetic flourish; he was stripping away the interpretive haze that magnifies fear. A pounding heart becomes "I notice my heart rate is elevated," not "I'm about to have a breakdown." A tense meeting becomes "I am in a discussion with competing interests," not "They're all against me." This linguistic precision disrupts the mind's automatic fusion of sensation with catastrophe. Labelling serves as a cognitive speed bump, slowing down the mental acceleration that can turn a transient physiological change into a sustained panic. It also reduces the brain's tendency to overgeneralise—recognising that you are feeling *social anxiety* before giving a presentation is fundamentally different from deciding you are an *inherently anxious person*.

Once the experience is labelled, the next move is to Locate. Anxiety thrives in vagueness; it resists being pinned to a specific time, place, and trigger. Locating forces the brain to define the threat in concrete coordinates, which can often reveal that the scope is far smaller than it feels. This can mean literally orienting yourself in the environment—naming what you can see, hear, and touch—or identifying the exact moment in the sequence of events where discomfort began. For example, a surgeon noticing a surge of tension during a complex operation might recognise that it began not with the procedure itself, but with an unfamiliar piece of equipment. This shift from "everything is going wrong" to "I am adjusting to one new variable" reduces the perceived scale of the threat, and with it, the sense of helplessness. In everyday contexts, Locating might involve narrowing a diffuse fear of "career failure" down to a single upcoming performance review, or realising that the anxiety began after a single ambiguous email. The act of locating transforms an amorphous cloud of dread into a defined event—one you can plan for, respond to, or, in some cases, set aside entirely.

The third step, Limit, introduces containment. Left unchecked, anxiety loops sprawl, consuming mental bandwidth and physical energy far beyond the proportion of the trigger. Limiting is the deliberate setting of boundaries on how much attention, time, or behavioural change you will give to the anxiety. This might take the form of a temporal limit—deciding to revisit the problem after a meeting rather than in the middle of it—or a procedural limit, such as writing down the worry once and refusing to mentally rehearse it again until a designated review period. In clinical settings, such boundaries are often referred to as "stimulus control" or "scheduled worry," but here the Stoic framing is equally relevant: you are asserting governance over what deserves your time. Limiting also guards against the subtle self-sabotage of over-preparation, where trying to control every variable becomes another form of avoidance. A person preparing for a challenging conversation might, for example, allow themselves twenty minutes of focused preparation, then refuse further mental rehearsal, knowing that beyond that point, each repetition fuels anxiety rather than readiness.

The final step, Lean In, confronts the core driver of most anxiety loops: avoidance. Avoidance temporarily reduces discomfort, but over time it trains the mind and body to treat the avoided situation as inherently dangerous. Leaning in is not about plunging recklessly into worst-case scenarios, but about making a deliberate, proportionate approach toward the feared situation or sensation. In practice, this may mean holding your ground in the meeting where you want to escape, or allowing the physical sensations of anxiety to rise without rushing to neutralise them. The principle is one of controlled exposure: by staying present in the discomfort, you teach your nervous system that the situation can be endured without catastrophe. This echoes the Stoic practice of voluntary hardship—engaging with manageable difficulty to build resilience before larger trials demand it. Importantly, leaning in is not an end in itself; it is the mechanism that converts the preceding steps from cognitive exercises into behavioural change. Without it, Label, Locate, and

Limit remain theoretical; with it, they become embodied actions that shift the trajectory of the loop.

The elegance of this four-step process lies in its portability and scalability. It can be run in under a minute when you are standing in a lift, feeling a sudden rise in tension, or extended over hours in the context of a complex, evolving challenge. It requires no equipment, no special setting, and no external validation. A military officer might use it under fire, moving through the steps in rapid sequence to stabilise focus; a parent might use it at the dinner table, silently cycling through the process before addressing a tense family conversation. Its adaptability makes it not merely a crisis tool but a daily practice. Over time, repeated application builds fluency—the steps become automatic, executed before the loop gains momentum.

However, its effectiveness is contingent on deliberate practice, not just intellectual understanding. Knowing the sequence without applying it is akin to memorising the layout of a parachute without ever jumping. The skill is forged in the act of using it—preferably first in low-stakes situations, so that the process is familiar when pressure rises. Like all Stoic tools, it is not about perfection but about direction: each run-through, whether smooth or halting, is an act of reclaiming agency from the automatic circuits of anxiety. When used consistently, the four steps do more than interrupt individual loops—they begin to recondition the underlying reflexes, making calm a trained response rather than an accidental occurrence. The anxiety loop may never disappear entirely, but with this method, it no longer dictates the terms.

Integrating All Skills

The true measure of any self-mastery framework is not how well it performs in theory, but how seamlessly it operates in the friction of real life. Anxiety management tools are often learned in isolation—breathing techniques in one session, cognitive reframing in another, exposure principles in yet another—but crises rarely arrive in neat categories. When uncertainty accelerates, you do not have the luxury of consulting a mental catalogue, flipping between index cards marked "physical regulation," "mindset shift," or "behavioural strategy." You need an integrated response, where the skills you've practised align into a single, coordinated act. This is the difference between knowing *about* resilience and embodying it.

In the same way that a trained pianist no longer thinks about finger placement but simply plays, an effective anxiety responder moves fluidly between tools, guided not by rigid sequence but by situational need. A paramedic, for example, arriving at the scene of a traffic accident, might instinctively apply grounding techniques to manage their own rising adrenaline, simultaneously deploy assertive communication to coordinate bystanders, and draw on exposure training to remain within the distressing environment without retreating. None of these steps is executed in isolation; they interlock, each reinforcing the other's effect. *This is the art of integration—making the skills indistinguishable from the self.*

The challenge is that most people stop at competence in individual tools without practising the transitions between them. They can execute controlled breathing in a quiet room, recall Stoic maxims while reading philosophy, or set exposure hierarchies on paper. But when they face a demanding client, a hostile boardroom, or a sudden health scare, those skills remain compartmentalised, like unused gear in separate drawers. Integration begins by training those transitions deliberately. For instance, pairing a labelling exercise with immediate physiological regulation ensures that cognitive clarity is reinforced by a calmer bodily state, preventing the kind of mental drift that can pull you back into the anxiety loop.

Integration also means recognising that earlier tools in this book were never intended as stand-alone fixes. Each was a part of a larger operating system. The Weekly Reckoning sharpens your ability to detect avoidance patterns; that feeds directly into the Lean In step of the Stoic Loop Breaker. Celebrating Discomfort as Data conditions you to view anxiety spikes not as personal failures but as performance feedback; that mindset ensures you enter the Limit stage of the loop breaker with less resistance. Acute Calm Protocol provides a rapid triage method for moments of panic, which can then be expanded into deeper recovery using Aftershock Recovery techniques. Seen in isolation, each skill is valuable. Used in sequence, they form a closed feedback loop—detect, intervene, act, reinforce—that continuously builds capacity.

One of the most powerful benefits of integration is adaptability across intensity levels. The same interconnected framework that keeps you steady in a routine work presentation can scale to a high-stakes, life-altering moment. Consider a commercial airline pilot encountering unexpected turbulence severe enough to trigger passenger panic. Their acute calm skills manage their own physiological response; their agency-in-chaos training keeps decision-making clear under pressure; their anchoring in core beliefs—such as prioritising safety above all—guides tactical choices. Post-event, their aftershock recovery strategies prevent the experience from imprinting as lingering anxiety. This is not a string of unrelated tactics—it is a single, coherent response, assembled from well-rehearsed components.

However, integration is not purely about speed or efficiency. It is about *economy of effort*. By linking tools, you reduce redundant mental labour and avoid overreliance on any single strategy. If you try to calm anxiety solely through bodily regulation, without addressing cognitive patterns, you risk temporary relief without long-term change. If you focus only on reframing thoughts without grounding the body, you may sustain an intellectual argument with yourself while your nervous system remains in full alarm. Integration resolves this mismatch by addressing multiple dimensions simultaneously—physiological, cognitive, and behavioural—so they no longer work at cross-purposes.

Real-time integration also relies on an awareness of sequence. While it's tempting to think you can apply skills in any order, the timing of interventions matters. In a situation where anxiety is surging rapidly, physical regulation often precedes complex cognitive work, simply because a flooded nervous system has less capacity for nuanced thinking. In contrast, in a slower-burning anticipatory anxiety, cognitive labelling and reframing might be the entry point, followed by strategic behavioural engagement. Practising different sequences in low-stakes environments allows you to develop the flexibility to choose the right order under pressure, rather than defaulting to the one you happen to remember.

Case studies illustrate the transformative potential of integration. A search-and-rescue volunteer described how, during a mountain recovery mission, they moved seamlessly between locating the source of their anxiety (a sudden change in weather conditions), limiting its scope (deciding to focus only on the immediate path rather than the entire descent), applying controlled breathing to maintain composure, and leaning in to the discomfort of uncertainty by continuing the mission step-by-step. They noted that what made the process effective was not the individual skills—each of which they had practised before—but the *unbroken chain of application*. There was no pause to decide "now I will regulate my breathing" or "now I will reframe my thoughts"; the skills had been integrated into instinct.

The work of integration is never "finished." Just as a musician keeps refining their ability to improvise, or an athlete continues to develop situational awareness, integrating anxiety management tools is an ongoing process. Each real-life application provides data: which sequence worked best, where the chain faltered, what skill was missing. The goal is not to rehearse for an imagined perfect performance, but to keep closing the gap between practice and reality until there is no gap at all.

Ultimately, integration is the point at which the tools stop feeling like external interventions and start becoming part of who you are. You are no longer "using a grounding exercise"—you are grounded. You are not "employing a reframing technique"—you are thinking clearly. This shift from doing to being is the hallmark of mastery. And mastery, in this context, is not about never experiencing anxiety, but about ensuring it never hijacks your agency. Once all the earlier skills operate as a single, fluent system, anxiety becomes less of an adversary to battle and more of a signal to engage the process you already know by heart.

Scaling the Method

A method that cannot adapt to scale will inevitably fail the people who most need it. Anxiety is not a uniform experience; it is a spectrum, ranging from the faint but persistent hum of unease before a presentation to the full-force surge of physiological and cognitive overwhelm during a high-stakes emergency. A reliable loop-breaking framework must function across this range, offering a light-touch intervention for the mildest cases while delivering a decisive, high-intensity countermeasure when anxiety spikes beyond ordinary coping capacity. The Stoic Loop Breaker was never designed as a single-speed tool—it is meant to be adjusted like a precision instrument, capable of being dialled up or down according to situational demand.

Scaling begins with recognising that *intensity dictates execution.* At low anxiety levels, the method can be applied in a measured, almost conversational way with the self. You might label the anxious loop with gentle detachment, locate its source through quick reflection, limit its scope by reframing its relevance, and lean in with a small behavioural experiment. This is the preventative maintenance mode—subtle, efficient, and able to blend into the rhythm of ordinary life without creating disruption. In contrast, at high intensity, the same four steps must be enacted with a compressed timeline and amplified precision. The labelling becomes more direct and declarative, a verbal anchor to halt spiralling thought. Locating the source is stripped to essentials—no analytical deep dive, just identifying the dominant threat signal. Limiting becomes triage: focusing on the smallest actionable sphere of control. Leaning in becomes an act of deliberate exposure, measured in seconds rather than gradual progression.

Case studies make this distinction vivid. A junior barrister facing low-level anticipatory anxiety before court might apply the loop breaker over the course of an afternoon—labelling the unease as "standard pre-trial activation," locating it in the mind's rehearsal of possible questioning, limiting it by reminding themselves that professional competence is not defined by a single day's outcome, and leaning in by rehearsing opening remarks aloud in the office. Meanwhile, a soldier in an active engagement zone, hearing unexpected gunfire, has seconds to apply the same architecture: "Threat present" (label), "Sound direction east" (locate), "Secure cover and return visual" (limit), "Move towards objective under control" (lean in). Both follow the framework, but the scale, tempo, and depth differ radically.

One of the barriers to effective scaling is the human tendency to treat anxiety protocols as static scripts. When someone learns the loop breaker in a calm environment, they may fixate on executing it exactly as practised—step one in full, then step two, and so on. This rigidity is dangerous at high intensity, where time and cognitive bandwidth are compressed. To scale effectively, the method must be modular, capable of partial application without losing integrity. In extreme states, you might need to begin with limit before locate, if containment is the most urgent priority. Conversely, in mild situations, you might linger in locate and limit for reflective insight before leaning in. *Scaling is not about mechanical fidelity—it is about functional adaptability.*

Scaling also has a physiological dimension. In mild anxiety, your body's baseline state still allows for deliberate reasoning; in extreme anxiety, the sympathetic nervous system may overwhelm the prefrontal cortex. Understanding this difference is essential, because it shapes which tools pair most effectively with each step. At the mild end, cognitive techniques—such as reframing, probability testing, or Stoic premeditatio—can dominate. At the severe end, pairing steps with somatic regulation becomes critical; for example, labelling a panic onset aloud while simultaneously using tactical breathing to recover cognitive bandwidth. Without this physiological scaling, the loop breaker risks becoming purely intellectual—a model that works only when you already have enough calm to think clearly.

The method also scales socially. In everyday low-intensity scenarios, the loop breaker can be applied internally without external cues; no one else need know you are using it. But in extreme circumstances, scaling might require integrating others into the process. Crisis response teams often enact collective versions of these steps—labelling the situation in shared language ("We have a chemical spill in the south corridor"), locating its scope and threat zones, limiting exposure through containment measures, and leaning in by executing rehearsed interventions. The principles are identical, but the scale involves multiple minds, bodies, and coordinated actions.

A key skill in scaling is pre-identifying your personal intensity thresholds. Without this, it is easy to misjudge and under- or over-apply the method. People often over-engineer their response to mild anxiety, exhausting themselves, or under-commit in high-stakes situations, relying on steps that are too slow or superficial. Keeping a brief mental map of your scaling parameters—what mild, moderate, and severe anxiety look like in your body and mind—allows you to calibrate the method appropriately. This awareness is built not in the moment of crisis, but in repeated practice across different contexts, deliberately testing the loop breaker at various levels of stress to see how it holds.

It is also worth acknowledging that scaling demands an acceptance of imperfection. At high intensity, execution will never be as clean as it is in training; at low intensity, you might be tempted to skip steps entirely. The point of scaling is not flawless application but preservation of function—enough to stop the anxiety loop from tightening. This is why the method's durability lies in its simplicity: four steps, easily remembered, infinitely adjustable. They form a mental architecture strong enough to withstand compression yet flexible enough to expand into deeper work when time and clarity allow.

Ultimately, the strength of the Stoic Loop Breaker lies in its elasticity. It is not a ceremonial sequence to be wheeled out only in controlled settings; it is a living method, designed to adapt in pace, depth, and scope without losing coherence. In mild anxiety, it keeps you engaged and prevents drift into avoidance. In extreme anxiety, it keeps you moving when everything in your body wants to freeze. The principles never change, but their execution bends to meet the moment. That is what makes it not just a tool, but an operational philosophy—one that honours the Stoic ideal of control over the controllable, no matter the scale of the storm.

Case Study Walkthroughs

Anxiety is an abstract concept until you see it acted upon in the heat of reality. Theories can be memorised and frameworks neatly diagrammed, but their value lies in the moment when a person under genuine strain decides—often instinctively—to apply them. What follows are not neat textbook scenarios but real-world examples in which the Stoic Loop Breaker was used successfully, each shaped by the unpredictable nature of human stress and decision-making. They show the method not as an isolated intervention, but as a living tool that bends to circumstance while retaining its core logic.

Consider Sarah, a senior marketing executive preparing to present quarterly results to a board of directors who had recently expressed doubts about her department's direction. In the week leading up to the meeting, she experienced a steady build of anticipatory anxiety—tightness in her chest, trouble focusing, intrusive doubts about whether she would be challenged aggressively. In the past, she would have tried to suppress these sensations, which only seemed to amplify them. This time, she applied the loop breaker over the course of several days. She *labelled* the feeling explicitly—"This is performance anxiety, not evidence of incompetence." By naming it, she broke the reflexive loop of interpreting tension as danger. She then *located* its source with specificity: it was not the presentation content itself, but the fear of losing credibility in front of senior stakeholders. This clarity allowed her to *limit* the scope of the anxiety—she could not control their predisposition, but she could control her mastery of the data and her preparedness for difficult questions. Finally, she *leaned in* with structured exposure: she staged two rehearsal sessions with colleagues playing the role of a sceptical board, gradually raising the level of challenge. When the day came, the anxiety did not vanish, but it was harnessed into alertness. Her performance was sharper, not in spite of the adrenaline, but because she had worked with it instead of against it.

Contrast this with James, a firefighter responding to a high-rise blaze. Arriving on scene, he was told that two people were trapped on the top floor with no immediate stair access. His first surge was physiological—elevated heart rate, tunnel vision. In seconds, he *labelled* the state: "Adrenaline spike—stay operational." This concise, almost telegraphic identification prevented emotional overwhelm from dictating his next move. He *located* the problem spatially, identifying the floor and the most viable ladder positioning. The *limit* step in this context was not about emotional containment but about narrowing the tactical focus: prioritising the rescue route over secondary tasks. The *lean in* phase was immediate—ascending under hazardous conditions while applying breathing control to maintain clarity. Here, the loop breaker was not stretched across hours but compressed into a thirty-second operational decision cycle. The method's adaptability in this high-intensity, zero-margin environment illustrates its resilience when scaled to extreme conditions.

Then there is Amina, a postgraduate student in clinical psychology facing her first session with a patient presenting with severe trauma. Her anxiety manifested less as a physical surge and more as cognitive doubt—What if I make it worse? What if they see I'm inexperienced? She began by *labelling* these thoughts explicitly, externalising them as "novice therapist anxiety" rather than letting them masquerade as an assessment of her competence. She *located* the anxiety in her lack of direct trauma-handling experience, not in her general therapeutic skill. This allowed her to *limit* the reach of the fear—it was not about her entire career, but this particular interaction. Her *lean in* step was subtle: she entered the session and committed to maintaining presence for the full duration, resisting the temptation to overcompensate with excessive note-taking or scripted questions. By the end, she found that her anxiety had diminished not by suppression, but through embodied engagement with the role she had feared she could not inhabit.

One of the most revealing patterns across these cases is that *the four steps rarely unfold identically*. In Sarah's corporate context, the work was preparatory and stretched over time; for James, it was reactive and instantaneous; for Amina, it was sustained and relational. The steps adapt not only to intensity but also to the nature of the task—whether it is primarily cognitive, physical, or interpersonal. This flexibility underscores why rigid adherence to a single "correct" sequence undermines effectiveness. The loop breaker thrives in dynamic application, where the user's judgement tailors execution to the moment's demands.

It is equally important to note what these examples do not show: complete eradication of anxiety. In all three cases, the individuals still experienced physiological arousal or mental tension. The success lay not in eliminating the sensation but in changing the relationship to it—from adversary to operational signal. This is where the Stoic foundation becomes visible. By reframing anxiety as a neutral data point, the individual maintains agency, reduces reactive decision-making, and can choose responses aligned with their objectives and values.

Real-world application also reveals the critical role of *practice under varied conditions*. Sarah's earlier experiments with labelling and limiting in low-stakes meetings gave her fluency in the method when the high-stakes board presentation arrived. James' use of the loop breaker in live-fire drills meant he did not have to recall the steps consciously during the blaze—they emerged automatically, freeing cognitive bandwidth for situational analysis. Amina's deliberate rehearsals with simulated patients allowed her to experience and manage anticipatory anxiety in a controlled environment before applying the method in a genuine therapeutic exchange. This principle—that repeated, low-pressure engagement with the method strengthens high-pressure execution—is as relevant in academia as it is in military operations.

Finally, these walk-throughs show that the loop breaker is not confined to personal, internal management. In some cases, its logic can be extended to group dynamics. James' *label* step doubled as a team communication act; his verbal confirmation of the threat state informed his crew's coordination. Sarah's *locate* process benefited from a colleague's input, allowing her to refine her understanding of the board's likely objections. Even Amina, in the privacy of a therapy room, found that her leaning in created a calmer environment for the patient, who in turn responded with greater openness. When applied with awareness, the method not only breaks the individual anxiety loop but can also dampen the amplification of stress within a team or dyad.

Each of these scenarios affirms a central truth: the Stoic Loop Breaker is not a theoretical exercise, but a live instrument for navigating the varied landscapes of anxiety. Its success is measured not by the absence of discomfort, but by the preservation—and often the sharpening—of functional capacity in moments that would otherwise erode it. The case studies remind us that in practice, the method is less about reciting steps than about internalising a way of thinking: to name what is happening, to orient toward its source, to contain its spread, and to step deliberately into the space it threatens to close off. When this becomes second nature, the loop breaker moves from being an emergency measure to a companion skill—ready whenever the mind begins to spiral, whether in a boardroom, on a ladder, or in the quiet intensity of a conversation.

Chapter 13
Beyond Calm: Building a Stoic Life

Mastery seldom announces itself with fanfare; more often, it is the quiet accumulation of repeated effort, the persistence through days when novelty has worn thin and applause has long faded. In the realm of anxiety management, as in any demanding discipline, there is a seductive temptation to see breakthroughs as final destinations—"I no longer panic before presentations," or "I can travel without spiralling into dread." Yet the reality is more enduring, if less dramatic: what you achieve under pressure today must be reinforced with deliberate practice tomorrow. Skills neglected do not merely plateau—they regress. The nervous system, like any adaptive mechanism, reshapes itself according to repeated use. Absent intentional engagement, it slips back into its familiar grooves: avoidance, rumination, and reflexive over-control. Mastery, then, is less a milestone than an ongoing maintenance project.

Over time, the nature of this practice evolves. Early on, effort is primarily inward-facing—learning to weather your own storms, to navigate internal turbulence with grace. Yet as competence deepens, the vector of effort often extends outward. Teaching others the techniques you have honed is not merely an act of generosity; it reinforces your own mastery. Explaining labelling to a colleague or guiding a friend through the "limiting and leaning in" approach before their first public talk forces articulation of principles previously executed almost automatically. This conscious expression exposes blind spots, sharpens conceptual clarity, and cements habits more firmly. Instruction is not an adjunct to growth; it accelerates it. The Stoics recognised this: Marcus Aurelius's Meditations served simultaneously as self-reminder and philosophical discourse, proof that teaching and living well are inseparable.

Maintaining and transmitting skills opens the door to another critical shift: the gradual expansion of your circle of control. Early practice often confines application to narrowly defined challenges—a single meeting, a brief social exchange, a routine appointment. But remaining within these limited scenarios risks stagnation. A robust life requires the courage to scale challenges deliberately, increasing complexity or emotional stakes without tipping into overwhelm. Someone who remains composed in one-to-one conversations may next tackle small group discussions, then formal debates, eventually leadership roles. This is not about pursuing difficulty for its own sake; it is about reshaping a life no longer constrained by anxiety-driven boundaries. Paradoxically, calm emerges most reliably when it is treated as a byproduct of meaningful, value-driven action rather than the primary objective.

This reframing challenges much contemporary discourse, which positions tranquillity as the ultimate goal. Such a focus has two pitfalls: it cultivates hyper-vigilance about internal states—"Am I calm yet? Am I losing it?"—which fuels anxiety, and it sets one up for inevitable failure in high-pressure contexts. A soldier in combat, a surgeon mid-procedure, a parent in crisis—none can afford perfect emotional stillness. Yet all can exercise clarity, agency, and principled action despite intense arousal. When attention aligns with chosen values—courage, justice, contribution—calm often arrives unbidden, a secondary effect of refusing to be swept up in turbulence beyond control.

Viewed this way, constructing a Stoic life is less about sustaining a permanent internal climate than cultivating a dependable stance toward both external events and internal fluctuations. It involves recognising cycles of tension and release, preparation and recovery, and committing to practices that keep skills active and perspectives broad. The tools described here are not emergency devices to be dusted off once a year; they are instruments of living, deployed daily—sometimes conspicuously, often quietly, always available. Growth is measured not only by personal mastery over anxiety, but also by the stability, courage, and moral clarity you nurture in others.

This chapter takes that premise seriously. It moves beyond isolated tactics and momentary victories to explore embedding Stoic principles so deeply that they shape the architecture of life itself. You will see how consistent practice sharpens the edge, how teaching fortifies your own hand, how expanding your circle of control broadens engagement, and how calm—pursued indirectly—becomes a reliable companion rather than a fragile aspiration. The aim is to shift focus from surviving individual storms to cultivating a life that requires less rescue, marked by the quiet confidence of one who no longer fears their return.

Why Mastery Requires Maintenance – The ongoing nature of anxiety management

The paradox of mastery is that the moment you believe you have secured it is the moment it begins to slip away. This is as true for anxiety management as it is for playing an instrument, speaking a language, or maintaining peak physical fitness. Neural pathways, emotional regulation patterns, and behavioural habits are living processes, not fixed achievements. They require reinforcement, adaptation, and sometimes reinvention to remain functional in changing circumstances. The human nervous system is designed for efficiency, which means it will always revert to well-rehearsed patterns when under strain. If those patterns have historically been rooted in avoidance, hypervigilance, or catastrophic thinking, they will attempt to reassert themselves in moments of stress unless continuously countered by more constructive, practised alternatives. This is why individuals who have made significant progress in managing anxiety may still find themselves blindsided months or even years later if they neglect the ongoing work.

One of the most common misconceptions is that anxiety mastery is a singular, climactic transformation—that once you have "overcome" your symptoms, the work is finished. But anxiety is not a temporary virus to be eradicated; it is a set of interlinked physiological, cognitive, and behavioural tendencies that can be managed but not permanently deleted. The Stoic perspective recognises this not as a flaw or limitation but as a reality of the human condition. Just as a skilled pilot still performs pre-flight checks for every journey, no matter how many thousands of hours they have flown, so too must the anxiety practitioner maintain and recalibrate their mental and physical readiness. Consistency is not an admission of weakness; it is the architecture that prevents collapse.

Maintenance is also essential because the context in which anxiety emerges is never static. Personal circumstances evolve—relationships shift, careers change, health fluctuates—and each new chapter presents different triggers and demands. A person who has mastered their anxiety around workplace performance may still be destabilised by a sudden bereavement or a geopolitical crisis that alters their sense of safety. Moreover, external pressures are often subtle, cumulative, and not immediately recognised until they erode resilience. For example, an emergency physician who has successfully managed years of high-pressure clinical work might still find their composure unravelling after prolonged exposure to systemic understaffing, administrative chaos, and political interference in healthcare. Without deliberate maintenance, these shifts accumulate silently until they become overwhelming.

There is also a deeper, more philosophical reason why mastery requires continual attention: emotional regulation is a skill that interacts with one's moral and existential orientation. The Stoics understood that tranquillity was not simply the absence of distress but the alignment of perception, intention, and action with one's principles. This alignment is not set-and-forget; it demands ongoing reflection, recalibration, and honest self-assessment. Without such work, complacency sets in, and old habits creep back under the guise of confidence. People who cease deliberate practice often fail not because they encounter a stronger wave of anxiety, but because they have gradually lost the reflexes and perspective that once kept them afloat.

Real-world examples bear this out. Consider elite athletes who retire at the height of their game and then attempt to return years later. Their technical skills may still be present, but their reflexes, endurance, and mental conditioning have dulled. In anxiety management, the equivalent might be the executive who, after years of daily mindfulness and reflective journaling, gradually drops these practices when the pressure subsides. For a while, nothing seems amiss—until an unforeseen crisis triggers a cascade of overthinking, insomnia, and panic that feels eerily like the past they thought was behind them. This is not evidence that the earlier tools "failed"; it is evidence that the ongoing training that kept those tools sharp has been neglected.

From a neurobiological standpoint, the argument for maintenance is clear. Neural pathways strengthen with repeated use and weaken when unused—a principle known as synaptic plasticity. When you repeatedly apply grounding techniques, cognitive reframing, or controlled breathing during moments of discomfort, you are reinforcing the circuitry that allows those responses to be automatic. Conversely, when you allow long gaps between practice, those same circuits become less responsive, and older anxiety pathways can reassert dominance. Maintenance is, therefore, less about holding the line against relapse and more about ensuring that your mental and physical systems remain primed to respond constructively under varied and unpredictable conditions.

There is also the question of skill integration. Many people begin anxiety management with discrete tools—breathing exercises, thought labelling, body scans, or exposure hierarchies—and apply them in isolated contexts. Over time, mastery comes from integrating these tools into a fluid, adaptive response. This integration only deepens through repetition across different scenarios. If you stop using these tools outside of acute distress, you lose not only the individual techniques but also the synergy that allows them to be deployed instinctively in high-stakes moments. A firefighter does not wait for a blaze to practise with equipment; drills in safe environments ensure that when the alarm sounds, every motion is automatic.

Critically, the maintenance of mastery is not solely about rehearsal—it is about evolution. The anxiety you faced at 25 will not be identical to the anxiety you face at 45. Your triggers, context, and responsibilities will change, and so must your approach. For instance, someone who initially overcame social anxiety in their twenties by building public speaking confidence may find that in midlife, their primary anxiety revolves around their teenager's wellbeing or their parents' declining health. The core tools remain relevant, but they must be adapted to the different emotional textures and practical demands of these new challenges. Without this adaptability, tools that once felt liberating can start to feel irrelevant or even inadequate.

A useful way to think about maintenance is to see it as a multi-layered process. At the most immediate level, it involves daily habits that keep your body and mind in balance—sleep hygiene, exercise, reflective practice, and meaningful social contact. At the intermediate level, it means regular exposure to manageable challenges that keep your anxiety-regulation systems active without overwhelming them. And at the broader level, it requires a deliberate alignment of your life's direction with values that prevent chronic dissonance—because no amount of breathing exercises will compensate for a life lived in persistent violation of one's conscience. This layered approach ensures that maintenance is not a chore tacked onto life, but an integrated part of living well.

Ultimately, the need for maintenance is not a mark of fragility but of realism. A Stoic approach recognises that human beings are not static; our environments, bodies, and internal landscapes shift constantly. Mastery in anxiety management is therefore not a trophy to be displayed but a practice to be renewed—daily, deliberately, and with humility. The reward for this ongoing work is not merely the absence of anxiety spikes but the presence of a deeper, more reliable steadiness that can withstand the inevitable unpredictabilities of life. That steadiness is not given; it is built, rebuilt, and sustained over time, in the quiet, unglamorous discipline that true mastery demands.

Teaching Others the Tools – How sharing methods reinforces your own skill

The surest test of whether you understand something is whether you can teach it to someone else without dilution or confusion. This principle applies with particular force to anxiety management. Explaining a method to another person—especially someone who is anxious in that moment—requires a level of clarity, confidence, and adaptability that exposes the gaps in your own mastery. What you cannot explain succinctly, you do not fully command. What you cannot adapt to another's unique situation, you do not yet own as a flexible skill. Teaching transforms you from a passive user of tools into an active custodian of them, forced to recall, refine, and re-embed them into your own thinking.

The psychological mechanism behind this is well-documented. Known as the "protégé effect," the act of teaching increases retention, deepens conceptual understanding, and improves the ability to apply knowledge in varied contexts. When you instruct someone else in a breathing technique, cognitive reframe, or structured exposure strategy, you are not simply transmitting information; you are also rehearsing the skill yourself. You are forced to articulate why it works, anticipate objections, and address nuances that might otherwise remain unconscious. In doing so, you strengthen your own neural pathways associated with that skill, making it more readily accessible when you need it under pressure.

Beyond the cognitive benefit, there is a physiological one. Teaching another person how to remain calm requires you to model calmness yourself. A trembling voice or hurried delivery undermines your credibility and effectiveness, so you instinctively begin regulating your own breath, posture, and tone. This reciprocal effect—where the teacher embodies the lesson—means that each teaching moment is also a practice session in self-regulation. A firefighter explaining evacuation protocols to a new recruit unconsciously reinforces their own procedural memory; likewise, someone guiding a friend through grounding exercises is also rehearsing their own composure.

There is also a moral dimension. Sharing anxiety management tools creates a sense of responsibility for the wellbeing of others, which can strengthen your own discipline. If you have told a colleague to pause and name their thoughts before reacting, you will feel a sharper dissonance if you later ignore that same principle yourself. This social accountability can act as a guardrail, preventing complacency. In Stoic terms, teaching becomes a form of living in accordance with virtue—aligning your actions with what you have declared to be right and useful. The philosopher Epictetus, who taught that education was not about memorising doctrines but embodying them in conduct, would recognise in this process the mutual reinforcement of self and other.

Real-world examples illustrate how teaching reinforces mastery in high-pressure contexts. Military instructors often find their own discipline sharpened by the act of training recruits. A soldier who once learned to control panic during live fire will find that explaining the step-by-step process to a trainee not only refreshes their own memory but forces them to distil complex instincts into teachable components. The same occurs in healthcare: an experienced trauma nurse explaining triage priorities to a student nurse must mentally walk through each decision point, making their own process explicit and therefore more conscious and resilient under stress.

The process of teaching also reveals blind spots. When you attempt to guide someone through a grounding technique and they ask, "But what if I'm too agitated to even start counting my breaths?" you are compelled to think beyond the basic script. This prompts you to consider contingency steps you may never have needed personally but which expand your own competence. In effect, every question from a learner is a mirror showing you where your own skill set can grow. Over time, this questioning builds a more flexible, situationally aware mastery than solitary practice alone can achieve.

Teaching anxiety management tools is also an exercise in empathy, which itself strengthens the skill. You must step outside your own frame of reference and enter the mental world of someone whose anxiety may manifest differently to yours. Perhaps your own triggers are tied to performance evaluation, while theirs arise in crowded public spaces. In explaining the same method to them, you adapt the framing, examples, and pacing to fit their lived reality. This adaptability is a form of mastery: it proves that you understand the principle well enough to translate it across contexts, not simply to replicate it in your own.

There is a subtle but important shift that happens when you move from being solely a practitioner to also being a teacher. You begin to think less in terms of "what works for me" and more in terms of "what works, and why." The "why" matters because it connects the specific tool to underlying principles—principles that can be recombined and applied in new situations. For example, if you know that slow exhalation works because it stimulates the vagus nerve and activates the parasympathetic nervous system, you can apply that knowledge not just to breathwork but also to other calming activities that involve controlled exhalation, such as humming, chanting, or certain yoga poses. Teaching forces you to make these links explicit, thereby widening your own repertoire.

The reinforcing effect of teaching extends beyond one-to-one instruction. Public speaking, workshops, and even informal group discussions amplify the benefit by requiring you to organise your knowledge into coherent, sequential narratives. In doing so, you see your tools not as isolated techniques but as parts of an integrated system. This systems-level perspective is vital for handling complex, layered anxiety scenarios in real life. A police negotiator, for instance, cannot rely on a single de-escalation phrase; they must be able to weave multiple techniques together seamlessly, just as an experienced teacher of anxiety tools learns to connect breathwork, reframing, and situational awareness into a fluid sequence.

Of course, teaching carries its own risks. There is a temptation to slip into a performative role—speaking authoritatively while neglecting one's own internal state. It is possible to "talk a good game" while privately slipping back into counterproductive habits. This is where humility and self-monitoring become essential. The most effective teachers are those who remain conscious that they, too, are always in training. The act of teaching should not be seen as a graduation from learning but as a deeper form of it. Each time you explain, demonstrate, or troubleshoot a technique, you are in effect running a live-fire drill on your own capacity to apply it.

There is also the benefit of emotional contagion in reverse. Anxiety is socially contagious, but so is calm. When you teach and model these tools, you project a steadiness that can alter the emotional tone of the space you share with others. Over time, this feedback loop can solidify your own baseline composure: the more people expect you to be the "calm one," the more likely you are to inhabit that role naturally. While this should not become a source of pressure or an inauthentic mask, it can serve as a useful anchor in moments where your own anxiety threatens to resurface.

In the Stoic framework, the act of teaching is more than a pedagogical tool—it is a moral duty. Marcus Aurelius wrote extensively in his private reflections about his obligation to live in a way that benefited others, knowing that such service also reinforced his own virtue. Teaching anxiety management tools is a modern expression of that principle. It not only equips others to suffer less but also compels you to embody the qualities you advocate. In doing so, you are no longer just managing your own anxiety; you are contributing to a broader culture of composure and resilience, which in turn supports your own ongoing practice.

Teaching, then, is not an optional flourish for those who have "made it" in their anxiety journey—it is one of the surest ways to keep that journey alive and evolving. Every explanation is a rehearsal. Every demonstration is a drill. Every question from a learner is an opportunity to deepen and adapt your skill. In sharing the tools, you keep them sharp; in keeping them sharp, you ensure they will be there not only for those you teach, but for yourself, when the next wave comes.

Expanding the Circle of Control – Gradually tackling bigger challenges over time

A common trap in anxiety management is mistaking stability for progress. When we first learn to regulate our thoughts and physiological responses, we often cling to the routines and environments in which we feel safe. This is understandable—early stability is hard-won and can feel precarious—but it carries the risk of stagnation. The purpose of gaining control over anxiety is not to construct a smaller, more manageable world and stay there indefinitely. It is to enlarge the scope of what we can influence without being overwhelmed. This process, *expanding the circle of control*, is a deliberate, structured stretching of our capacities over time, moving from small, contained challenges towards more complex, unpredictable ones, without sacrificing the composure we have built.

The Stoics, from whom much of the philosophical foundation of this method is drawn, placed immense emphasis on distinguishing between what is within our control and what is not. But they did not intend this as a static distinction; rather, they saw it as a living practice. The more competent and resilient we become, the more we can handle within that circle. A novice sailor starts by managing a small boat on calm waters, but as skill and judgement deepen, they can navigate larger vessels through unpredictable seas. This expansion does not mean believing we can control *everything*—that is hubris—but it does mean that through repeated training and incremental exposure, the number of situations in which we can act effectively grows.

The danger of remaining at the same level of challenge is twofold. First, without exposure to variability and difficulty, skills atrophy.

Techniques that once felt sharp become rusty, not because they no longer work, but because they are no longer applied under pressure. Second, a static comfort zone can shrink over time. If we never step beyond it, the threshold for what feels threatening can lower, making previously manageable situations feel daunting again. The paradox of resilience is that it must be exercised against resistance. Just as muscles grow through progressive overload, emotional steadiness strengthens through facing—and mastering—increasingly demanding scenarios.

The practical question is how to expand the circle of control without triggering a collapse into old anxiety loops. The answer lies in structured progression. The leap from controlled breathing in a quiet room to delivering an unplanned speech to a large audience is too abrupt; the nervous system reads it as a threat rather than a challenge. Instead, incremental steps are essential. If public speaking is the ultimate goal, one might begin by expressing opinions in small meetings, then answering questions in slightly larger groups, then rehearsing a short talk in front of trusted peers, and only then moving towards more formal, high-stakes presentations. Each stage is challenging enough to require focus and self-regulation but not so overwhelming that it risks undoing previous progress.

This principle applies beyond individual skill-building. In organisational contexts, leaders often face a similar expansion. A manager who has learned to handle conflict calmly within a small team can extend that capacity to cross-departmental disputes, then to negotiations with external stakeholders, and eventually to crisis management at the organisational level. The same tools—maintaining composure, clarifying facts, focusing on controllable actions—are applied at increasing scales. The key is that each new challenge is deliberately chosen, not stumbled into, and met with conscious application of the methods already mastered.

There is also a psychological shift that occurs as the circle expands: a move from defensive control to generative control. Early anxiety management is often reactive—we learn to stop spirals, to recover from sudden shocks. As competence grows, the focus shifts towards using our stability proactively to create opportunities, solve problems, and influence events before they become crises. This generative mode of control requires a willingness to engage with more variables and more uncertainty. It is in this phase that calm stops being merely the absence of panic and becomes an enabling condition for purposeful action.

Real-world examples illustrate how this plays out. Consider an individual who initially struggles with social anxiety to the point of avoiding gatherings entirely. Early success might involve attending a brief, low-pressure event and managing to stay for an hour without distress. Over months, they might progress to hosting a small dinner, then joining a professional networking event, and later leading a public seminar in their area of expertise. By the final stage, the same individual who once viewed social situations as threats now actively uses them to further personal and professional goals. Importantly, this transformation was not the result of sudden boldness but of methodical expansion, each step consolidating the gains of the last.

There will inevitably be setbacks in this process. Not every attempt to expand control will succeed on the first try. Sometimes, the chosen challenge will exceed current capacity, triggering a spike in anxiety. This is not failure; it is data. By analysing what caused the overload—whether it was a gap in preparation, a misjudgement of difficulty, or an unexpected variable—we can recalibrate the progression. The ability to extract constructive insight from these moments is itself a marker of mastery, turning apparent reversals into part of the forward movement.

One of the subtler benefits of gradually expanding control is that it changes self-identity. We stop defining ourselves by our avoidance patterns or our sensitivity to triggers and start seeing ourselves as capable, adaptable actors in a wider range of situations. This identity shift reinforces the behavioural gains, making it more likely that we will seek new challenges rather than retreat from them. The circle of control, then, is not just an external map of what we can handle—it becomes an internal map of who we believe ourselves to be.

From a Stoic standpoint, the expansion process also deepens our understanding of what *cannot* be controlled. Exposure to bigger challenges brings us into contact with more factors outside our influence. This could seem discouraging, but in practice it sharpens discernment. We become more adept at directing energy towards what can be changed and releasing what cannot. The irony is that the broader our control becomes, the less we waste time trying to control the uncontrollable. This combination—expanded capacity and refined focus—is what allows calm to be sustained even in high-stakes, high-uncertainty environments.

Ultimately, the disciplined expansion of the circle of control is not about perpetual escalation for its own sake. It is about ensuring that our capacity keeps pace with the demands of life, so that the skills we have built do not calcify in conditions that no longer reflect reality. Anxiety thrives in the gap between challenge and capacity. By closing that gap through gradual, deliberate exposure to bigger challenges, we keep anxiety in check not just for the situations we face today, but for those we cannot yet foresee. The process requires patience, humility, and persistence—but the reward is a life in which composure and competence grow together, enabling us to meet more of the world on our own terms.

Calm as a Byproduct of Living Well – Positions calm not as the end goal, but the result of aligned, courageous living

The pursuit of calm, when made an end in itself, often fails. This is not because calm is unattainable, but because it is a secondary phenomenon—an emergent property of something deeper. When calm becomes the primary objective, people tend to grasp for it through avoidance, withdrawal, and the artificial dampening of emotion. These strategies may bring temporary relief, but they rarely yield lasting stability. *True calm arises not from fleeing discomfort, but from living in deliberate alignment with values, acting courageously in the face of uncertainty, and accepting the inherent volatility of life without being hostage to it.*

Modern culture frequently frames calm as a product one can purchase or a state one can schedule, from wellness retreats to mindfulness apps promising serenity in ten minutes a day. While these tools can have their place, they can also perpetuate the idea that calm is a possession—something that can be obtained and held on to if one finds the right technique or environment. The Stoic perspective, however, turns this on its head: calm is not a goal to be grasped but a companion that arrives naturally when one lives well. In this framing, the measure of success is not how serene you feel in a given moment, but how consistently you can act in accordance with your principles regardless of emotional turbulence.

This shift in perspective matters because a fixation on calm can paradoxically generate more anxiety. The moment calm is disrupted, a secondary fear emerges: *I'm losing my calm—this is bad.* This meta-anxiety often spirals faster than the original discomfort. But when calm is understood as a byproduct, its occasional absence is not a failure; it is simply feedback. If you are living in alignment—making choices grounded in what you believe to be right, engaging in meaningful work, investing in relationships of integrity—calm will tend to reassert itself over time, much like physical fitness returns when one maintains regular, appropriate exercise.

Living well in this sense requires the integration of courage. Without courage, values remain abstract ideals, easily deferred in the name of comfort. Courage operationalises values in the real world, where there are risks, losses, and unknowns. A physician who advocates for public health reforms in the face of political resistance may not feel calm in the moment—indeed, they may feel fear, frustration, and urgency—but their willingness to endure those states for the sake of a larger purpose makes them more resilient. Over time, this resilience fosters a deeper calm: not the absence of challenge, but a readiness to face challenge without being undone by it.

This principle is visible in diverse domains. In elite sport, athletes who fixate solely on the absence of nerves before competition often underperform, because their energy is spent on suppression rather than execution. Those who accept the presence of nerves but channel their focus into executing their training under pressure tend to find that calm emerges mid-performance, as their actions align with their preparation and intent. Similarly, in professional negotiation, the most effective dealmakers are not those who appear perpetually relaxed, but those who can hold their ground and make principled decisions under tense conditions—calm is the residue of integrity in action, not the precondition for it.

Philosophically, this aligns with the Stoic distinction between preferred states and ultimate goods. Calm is a preferred state—pleasant and useful, but not in itself the foundation of a good life. The ultimate good, in their view, is living in accordance with virtue: wisdom, courage, justice, and self-discipline. When these are present, emotional steadiness tends to follow, but it is not the aim. This ordering of priorities prevents the endless chasing of mood states and redirects attention to what is under one's control: choices, actions, and attitudes.

It is worth noting that aligning life with values and exercising courage does not produce a constant, unbroken calm. Even the most disciplined and principled individuals experience agitation, grief, or anger. The difference lies in their relationship to those states—they do not treat them as threats to be eliminated, but as transient signals to be understood. This acceptance reduces the friction of emotional resistance, allowing equilibrium to re-establish itself more naturally. In contrast, those who pathologise every disruption to calm risk building a brittle form of stability, one that fractures easily under strain.

Case studies illustrate this with clarity. Consider a business founder navigating the collapse of a major contract. If calm were the explicit goal, the immediate instinct might be to retreat, to avoid confronting suppliers, employees, or investors until emotional composure returns. This may protect mood temporarily but can damage the enterprise irreparably. A founder operating from alignment and courage instead engages directly with stakeholders, acknowledges the difficulty, and initiates adaptive plans. This is not the easier path—it likely involves tense conversations and strategic uncertainty—but it is the one most likely to preserve integrity and create long-term stability. In such cases, calm often reappears not before or during the action, but in the reflective space afterwards, when one recognises that the essential things have been faced squarely.

The implications for anxiety management are profound. If calm is treated as a byproduct, one no longer needs to wait for it to act. Action becomes possible in the midst of discomfort, which in turn accelerates recovery and builds confidence. This contrasts sharply with the "calm-first" approach, which can trap individuals in extended avoidance while they attempt to manufacture the perfect internal state before engaging with life. The byproduct model fosters a bias towards action, grounded in values and tempered by reflection.

This reframing also dismantles the idea that a well-lived life is one without disturbance. Life inevitably contains volatility—economic downturns, personal loss, illness, conflict. If calm is defined as the absence of disturbance, it becomes incompatible with reality. If it is instead seen as the long-term residue of principled living, then disturbances are not disqualifying; they are part of the terrain. In this sense, calm is less like a fragile glass ornament and more like a muscle—strengthened not by stillness, but by use.

Finally, positioning calm as a byproduct restores a sense of agency. While emotional states fluctuate according to countless factors beyond our control, the alignment of our actions with our principles remains within reach in almost any circumstance. This means that the pathway to calm does not depend on waiting for conditions to improve or others to behave differently. It depends on living in a way that you would respect even under stress. Over time, the knowledge that you act consistently with your values creates a background stability that is less vulnerable to situational shocks.

When understood in this way, calm is no longer a delicate prize to be chased and guarded. It becomes the quiet strength that follows a life lived with clarity, courage, and coherence—a natural consequence of meeting the world on your own terms, not in the absence of fear, but in the refusal to be ruled by it.

About the Author

Rowan Mercer writes practical, evidence-aware guides that bridge ancient wisdom and modern psychology. Known for a calm, clear voice and field-tested exercises, Rowan focuses on helping readers face uncertainty without avoidance, build discomfort tolerance, and act on their values under pressure. Years of close work with everyday strivers—teachers, founders, parents, first-time managers—shaped Rowan's conviction that steadiness is a trainable skill, not a personality trait. When not writing, Rowan refines simple daily rituals—brief audits, breathing drills, and "courage reps"—that turn stressful moments into opportunities for agency. Rowan's mission is straightforward: make Stoic principles usable at 7:15 a.m. on a hard Monday, not just admirable on the page.

www.ingramcontent.com/pod-product-compliance
Lightning Source LLC
Chambersburg PA
CBHW031345230926
51848CB00002B/396